DEVELOPING GAMES THAT LEARN

Developing Games That Learn

Leonard Dorfman
Narendra K. Ghosh

MANNING

Greenwich
(74° w. long.)

The publisher offers discounts on this book when ordered in quantity. For more information please contact:

    Special Sales Department
    Manning Publications Co.
    3 Lewis Street
    Greenwich, CT 06830
    or
    73150.1431@compuserve.com
    Fax: (203) 661-9018

For updates regarding this book, see: http://www.browsebooks.com.

Copyediting: Margaret Marynowski
Typesetting: Stephen Brill
Cover Design: Fernando Gonzalez Bunster

 Copyright © 1996 by Manning Publications Co.
All rights reserved.

No part of this publication may be reproduced, stored in a retrieval system, or transmitted, in any form or by means, electronic, mechanical, photocopying, or otherwise, without prior written permission of the publisher.

♾ Recognizing the importance of preserving what has been written, it is the policy of Manning Publications to have the books they publish printed on acid-free paper, and we exert our best efforts to that end.

Many of the designations used by manufacturers and vendors to distinguish their products are protected as trademarks. Wherever these designations appear in this book, and we have been aware of the trademark claim, they have been typeset in initial caps or all caps.

Library of Congress Cataloging in Publication Data

Dorfman, Len.
    Developing games that learn / Leonard Dorfman, Narendra K. Ghosh.
      p.   cm.
    Includes index.
    ISBN 1-884777-15-5 (soft)
    1. Computer games — Programming.   2. Electronic digital computers — Programming.   3. Artificial intelligence.   I. Ghosh, Narendra K.   II. Title.
QA76.76.C672D67   1996
794.8'1631—dc20
                                                  96-146
                                                    CIP

1 2 3 4 5 6 7 8 9 10 — CR — 00 99 98 97 96

Printed in the United States of America

dedications

To Marc Neuberger, for his friendship and support with this project.

To Barbara, my wife of a quarter century in this lifetime, and to Rachel, our daughter, for being the radiant lights that brighten my life.

—Len

To my parents, Arup and Vinita, for their continual love and support, and to my sister, Nandita, for being everything a sister could be.

—Narendra

contents

Dedications v

About the authors xii

Introduction xiii

1 What is objective artificial intelligence? 1

1.1 A brief model of human consciousness 2

1.2 A brief model of program consciousness 4

1.3 Additional complications 5

1.4 Objective artificial intelligence 6
   Program instinct 7, Program learning 7, Program consciousness 7

1.5 OAI suitability query 7
   Is there any benefit from demonstrating humanlike performance? 8, What do you want the program to learn? 8, What is the nature of the demonstrated learning's quantifiable results? 9

1.6 OAI implementation overview 9
   Problem statement 10, OAI analysis 11, OAI design 11

1.7 Summary 12

2 Case study—Tic Tac Toe 13

2.1 Suitability query 14

2.2 OAI implementation overview of Tic Tac Toe 14
   Problem statement 14, Analysis 14, Analysis discussion 15, Design 15, Design discussion 15

2.3 Tic Tac Toe version 1 16

2.4 Tic Tac Toe version 2 29

2.5 Tic Tac Toe version 3 31

2.6 Summary 48

3 Drop Four case study overview and analysis 49

3.1 Four-in-a-row genre games 50

3.2 Drop Four case study 51

3.3 Drop Four's OAI suitability query 51
   Is there any aspect of the program which will benefit from humanlike performance? 51, What do you want your program to learn? 52, What is the nature of Drop Four's demonstrable learning? 52

3.4 OAI implementation overview of Drop Four 52
   Drop Four problem statement 52, Drop Four analysis (branch 1) 53, Drop Four analysis (branch 2) 53, Analysis discussion 53, Analyzing Drop Four program instinct 54

3.5 Summary 59

4 OAI design of Drop Four 61

4.1 Transition from analysis to design 61
   Design—branch 1 61, Design—branch 2 62

4.2 Historical notes 62
   Analyzing Drop Four program learning—move list data 63, Reality intervenes 65, Analyzing Drop Four program learning—memory markers 66, Reality intervenes 66, A return to marker analysis 67

4.3 Selecting programming environment and tools 67
   Designing Drop Four game play features 68, Designing move selection sequence 68, Designing Drop Four program instinct 69, Designing Drop Four program learning 70

4.4 Summary 71

5 Drop Four's DOS platform move selection 73

   5.1 Define statements and function map 73
   5.2 In the beginning 80
   5.3 Summary 99

6 Drop Four program instinct: Basic concepts mediating move generation 101

   6.1 The `coffin[]` array 102
   6.2 The `init_coffin()` function 105
   6.3 The `create_coffin(turn)` function 105
   6.4 The `create_coffin_o(opponent)` function 108
   6.5 The `create_win_board()` function 110
   6.6 The `coffin_pattern(turn)` function 111
   6.7 The `coffin_corner( UCHAR turn )` function 113
   6.8 Summary 114

7 Drop Four program instinct: Move decision scheme 115

   7.1 The `get_computer_move_first(...)` function 115
   7.2 Summary 143

8 Drop Four program instinct: Ply searching 145

   8.1 Ply search data and functions 145
   8.2 Initializing ghost boards 148
   8.3 Relocating data between ghost boards 148
   8.4 Getting the number of pieces in a ghost column 149
   8.5 Determining double wins on ghost boards 150
   8.6 Determining wins on ghost boards 151
   8.7 Searching for winning positions in ghost boards 152
   8.8 Can Dr. Plopper win on the next move? 154
   8.9 Will Dr. Plopper have to block a human win? 155
   8.10 Can Dr. Plopper set up a forced win in two moves? 157

x CONTENTS

 8.11 Dr. Plopper stops a two-move win setup for the human 159

 8.12 Dr. Plopper blocks a two-ply fork by human 161

 8.13 Summary 163

9 Drop Four program instinct: Primitive pattern-matching 165

 9.1 Program instinct: non-ply positional moves 166

 9.2 Program instinct: opening book positional moves 167

 9.3 Program instinct: opening book defensive moves 171

 9.4 Program instinct: opening book offensive moves 191

 9.5 Summary 199

10 Drop Four program instinct: Advanced positional move generation 201

 10.1 In search of a general board position evaluation algorithm 201

 10.2 Searching for three-filled patterns on the board 202

 10.3 Searching for three-filled patterns on `ghost1` 203

 10.4 Returning a move which creates three-filled patterns 203

 10.5 General position evaluation 205

 10.6 Summary 227

11 Drop Four program learning: Analyzing a loss 229

 11.1 Adding a move to the move list 229

 11.2 First-move analysis 231

 11.3 Level-two analysis `opponent_type_move(...)` support function 233

 11.4 Second move analysis 234

 11.5 Second move computer analysis 235

 11.6 Offensive first move analysis 236

 11.7 Offensive second move analysis 237

11.8 Offensive second move computer analysis 238

11.9 Implementation of marker disruption via
`first_pat_analysis(...)` 239

11.10 Adding a three-filled marker record and mirror to the
program subconscious 250

11.11 Summary 252

12 Drop Four program learning: Implementation 253

12.1 Finding winning patterns 253

12.2 Learning is demonstrated via `first_move_check(...)` 256

12.3 Learning is demonstrated via `second_move_check(...)` 258

12.4 Learning is demonstrated via `first_human_win(...)` 259

12.5 Learning is demonstrated via `second_human_win(...)` 260

12.6 Learning is demonstrated via
`off_first_human_win(...)` 262

12.7 Learning is demonstrated via `off_second_human_win(...)` 263

12.8 The `off_first_move_check(...)` function 265

12.9 The `off_second_move_check(...)` function 266

12.10 Summary 267

13 Transferring the program subconscious to and from disk and RAM 269

13.1 Transferring the program subconscious from hard disk to RAM 269

13.2 Transferring the program subconscious from RAM to hard disk 272

13.3 Summary 273

Epilogue 275

Index 277

about the authors

Leonard Dorfman, Ph.D., is the author of 22 computer science books, concentrating on C, C++, and Assembly language, a black comic novel, and four commercial software products. He has a strong background in educational research, and interest in psychology, philosophy, and Buddhist studies. He's a teacher and writer, and keeps shop at MultiGrain Solutions, a software development company.

Narendra K. Ghosh is currently obtaining a degree in computer science from Harvard University. He worked cooperatively with Len in developing Objective Artificial Intelligence and the learning algorithms, and in implementing the code used in the demonstration programs.

introduction

This easy-to-read book has been written specifically for professional programmers who wish to improve the performance of a program by giving it the facility to learn from its experiences. The learning algorithms and paradigm presented in this book are not intended to find a place within academe's enormous body of artificial intelligence literature. Rather, the paradigm and learning-based algorithms presented here were developed in the practical framework of commercial-based game design. Although the examples presented in this book are games, we believe that the paradigm and learning algorithms have application beyond the games arena.

The book begins by presenting a garden-variety look at consciousness, and follows with a definition of the objective artificial intelligence (OAI) paradigm. The OAI paradigm can be thought of as a higher level paradigm which resides above procedural and object-oriented paradigms. We believe that using the OAI paradigm may help you to begin thinking about ways in which you might develop new learning-based algorithms, or to modify one of the three learning-based algorithms we present in the book for use in your own programs.

The OAI paradigm guides programmers in developing programs which can learn from experience. However, we believe the nitty gritty of the algorithms which underlie what we call program learning to be unique to each situation. This view forces those who wish to use the OAI paradigm to delve deeply into the fundamental nature of the data. Your perception of the data will prove crucial in devising the algorithms which implement learning. It is our hope that using the OAI paradigm in program development may ease the creative and intellectual burdens of developing these specialized learning-based algorithms.

After introducing the theory underlying the OAI paradigm, we present a query procedure which you may find useful for determining if a programming project is a viable candidate for having its performance enhanced using learning-based algorithms. Although asking the right questions and defining the problem during the analysis process is often quite straightforward, developing OAI-based algorithms which will enhance your program's performance proves to be far more difficult.

The fruits of using OAI's analysis and design methodology can be evaluated by playing Drop Four, this book's featured demonstration program. Developed using the OAI paradigm, Drop Four selects moves in a humanlike time frame, and clearly demonstrates that it learns from its losses by not repeating the weak moves that prompted the losses in the first place. This fruitful adaptation most often takes place after a single loss.

Even though we would never claim that utilizing the OAI paradigm in your program development cycle might imbue your program with sentient consciousness, will power, or self awareness, we strongly encourage you to "play pretend" and imagine that it does. Imagine that the program you are building is indeed going to develop human abilities. We know that there are those in academe who will wince at this practice, and we respect their beliefs and cautions. That stated, we have nonetheless decided to encourage this behavior in the service of *fun*.

So go wild! Jump off the edge of the cliff! Drive ten miles an hour over the speed limit! And give a name to the portion of the code that makes decisions, responds and demonstrates learning. Anthropomorphize to the max.

In our case, we named Drop Four's decision making and learning code *Dr. Plopper*. When Dr. Plopper followed a loss by altering her/his play so as to eventually facilitate a wily win, we'd shout, "Dr. Plopper's Revenge!" We spoke in terms of Dr. Plopper's sleep disorder and alcohol issues after a slew of stupid moves. This proved to be quite fun and helpful in providing comic relief to the stress generated by struggling to find more robust implementations of program learning. ("Fun is good!"—Dr. Seuss.)

It is our hope that as you read through the text and work your way through the demonstration game's source code you will be able to discover wide-ranging application categories that can benefit from using OAI design methodologies. We hope that this work will provide a springboard for the development of learning-based algorithms.

Finally, although the main demonstration program is presented in C, the OAI program development methodology is not language specific.

What you need to use this book

Basically, you need to use your brain.

That stated, the demonstration programs presented in this book were compiled using Borland's 3.1 and 4.0 DOS compilers.

LEN DORFMAN and NARENDRA GHOSH

chapter 1

What is objective artificial intelligence?

This chapter begins by presenting a garden-variety model of human consciousness, and follows with our definition of *computer consciousness*. We do not claim that computer consciousness implies any form of self awareness or sentience. Rather, we frame this concept in the context of memory management because memory seems to play a pivotal role in learning.

Common sense indicates that human memory plays a role in one's ability to learn. Since we believe that computer memory plays a role in *program learning*, and since a computer's memory is more reliable than a human's, ultimately programs designed using the objective artificial intelligence (OAI) paradigm might be able to demonstrate abilities superior to those of a human. This view, of course, assumes that the algorithms underlying the computer's ability to learn are quite robust.

Interestingly, one reviewer of the manuscript's second draft (a Ph.D.-level academic familiar with much of the body of literature on artificial intelligence) took great umbrage at this comment. Although we appreciated his strenuous objection, we also know that the game program Drop Four has demonstrated the ability to improve its play, to the extent that it will exhibit strategy clearly superior to that of a human who has previously beaten it. The question as to how we should handle this claim arose.

To resolve the issue, let's take a careful look at Drop Four's behavior. For example, when Len installed a "fresh" version of Drop Four on his computer he could beat the game over 50% of the time. The learning algorithms kicked into gear (at the Advanced level of play) after each of his wins. Over time, Len's winning percentage dropped below 10% and Dr. Plopper's (the game's "brain") winning percentage approached 90%. Len became so demoralized that he began to hope for a draw. After all, a draw holds more dignity than a loss.

Something clearly happened to Dr. Plopper. Either Dr. Plopper learned from her/his losses and became a smarter, better Drop Four player, or Len became a less smart, weaker player. (This is not out of the realm of reason according to some of his friends!) This situation has been replicated by other players on their computers. In the end, we decided to suggest that you play the version of Drop Four supplied on the disk accompanying the book and decide for yourself. Although the mouse-based DOS character mode version of the user interface provided on the disk remains less slick than our OS/2 Presentation Manager version, the game plays just as smart. Play games of Drop Four when it's set at the Advanced level of play. Every time you beat Dr. Plopper, s/he will become smarter. Feel free to make your own decision about the veracity of our claim.

That stated, let's continue with our discussion of human and computer memory. In human terms, memory can be defined as the power to recall information representing past events. The term *memory markers* refers to the information retained in the mind after the process of losing certain details of an event has taken place. This loss of information seems to take place sometime between the initial experience and the process of remembering. Which information is lost and which is remembered is not completely under the person's control.

In contrast, *computer memory* refers to the ability to store and retrieve data stored in RAM or on a less volatile medium, such as a floppy or hard disk. All information that is stored in computer memory is under the programmer's control and can be retrieved with total accuracy. If the data that are stored in the computer's memory marker mesh well with the learning algorithms drawn from the OAI paradigm, the potential for learning is as powerful as a human's might be.

Taking a brief look at a model which outlines how a human's memory is managed can provide useful information for building a model of how computers can manage information. It is from this position that we began developing the memory management strategies outlined by OAI design methodology.

1.1 A brief model of human consciousness

At this time it might be useful to have a look at a brief model of human consciousness and see how it interacts with memory. In part, the models for human and computer

1.1 A BRIEF MODEL OF HUMAN CONSCIOUSNESS

Conscious mind
Subconscious mind
Unconscious mind
Sleep mind: dreaming
Sleep mind: nondreaming

Figure 1.1 The mind viewed as a spectrum of consciousness.

consciousness presented in this and the following section contain ideas drawn from the works of Ken Wilber[1] and Robert Orenstein[2].

We will use a spectrum model as a vehicle for presenting our garden-variety look at memory in the context of human consciousness. We will draw from the human spectrum model in looking at computer memory in the context of program consciousness.

Awareness may be thought of as a property of consciousness which imparts knowledge of the impressions generated by sensory input. Awareness exists only in the present moment. We can construct a view of the mind in which awareness is anchored tightly to the conscious stratum; see Figure 1.1.

In this model of the mind, the senses initially receive information and transfer it to the conscious stratum, where it is made available to the mind through awareness. The mind takes action on this information once awareness comes into play.

For the purposes of this book we'll primarily be looking at the conscious and subconscious strata and will touch briefly on the unconscious stratum. What follows is a focused look at the strata of consciousness which will be used as a basis in the development of selected OAI programming strategies. Table 1.1 gives an expanded view of the spectrum of consciousness.

An impression received by the conscious stratum can disappear when the sensory stimulus disappears. The sensory impression settles into the subconscious stratum. A sensory-generated impression remains in the subconscious stratum and is not known to the awareness residing in the conscious stratum because in our spectrum of consciousness, awareness is anchored in the conscious stratum.

---

1. Ken Wilber, *Spectrum of Consciousness*, Quest, CA (1977).
2. Robert Orenstein, *The Evolution of Consciousness*, Prentice-Hall, NY (1991).

Stratum	Qualities
Conscious	Receives impressions from the senses. The conscious stratum temporarily holds impressions and then releases them to the subconscious and unconscious strata.
Subconscious	Retains impressions for a while. Impressions can be recalled to the conscious stratum via will power. The conscious stratum has no knowledge of whether an impression remains in the subconscious until it tries to retrieve the impression via will power. The subconscious stratum may release impressions after a while.
Unconscious	Permanently retains impressions. Impressions can occasionally be recalled to the conscious stratum via hypnosis, dreams, metaphor and psychotherapy. Impressions to the unconscious stratum cannot be recalled via simple will power.

Table 1.1 An expanded view of the spectrum of consciousness.

A simple exercise might clarify this: stop reading right now and write down your home phone number. You'll most likely be able to write it down without much thought. Although you don't think about your home phone number all the time, you're able to easily call that information from your subconscious stratum via will power. Over time, some of the impressions in your subconscious stratum disappear. Imprints remain in the unconscious stratum. Once such an impression has left your subconscious stratum it may be brought to the conscious stratum via dream metaphors or other techniques.

1.2 *A brief model of program consciousness*

We conclude that computer programs may be thought of as being artificial because they are not imbued with humanlike self awareness or sentience and are programmed by humans or other computer programs. Although computer programs are artificial, we nonetheless believe that they provide an environment in which they can be viewed as having access to many strata of consciousness (memory). We will use the name *program consciousness* to describe all the memory that a program can utilize. Program consciousness is composed of both RAM and disk memory.

Stratum	Qualities
Program conscious	Temporarily holds data in RAM, and may take action by transferring the data to the subconscious stratum.
Program subconscious	Retains data impressions for a while. Impressions can be recalled to program conscious stratum via transfer of impressions (data records). Continues storing impressions until all the memory has been allocated. Hard disk memory which is automatically transferred to RAM after program launch is also defined as the program subconscious.
Program unconscious	Permanently retains impressions (data records) in files on hard disk. Impressions are rarely called to the conscious stratum, and only under clearly defined circumstances. Impressions are not available to the conscious stratum unless specialized circumstances exist. The data held on hard disk are not automatically transferred to RAM after program launch.

Table 1.2 A view of the spectrum of program consciousness.

As with humans, a program's consciousness can be viewed as being composed of different memory strata. Here's a look at how we layer the computer program's spectrum of consciousness (memory strata). Table 1.2 presents a view of the spectrum of program consciousness.

A computer program can create files of impressions and keep them in volatile memory, or can transfer them to storage media (hard disk drive, for example). The program can then search the file for the requested impression and retrieve it via disk I/O for use by the program's conscious stratum.

1.3 Additional complications

So far, the comparison between the spectrum of human consciousness and that of program conscious seems quite straightforward. In reality, however, that's not the case. A human most often lacks control over which information will be placed in the subconscious. The mind seems to place information in the subconscious automatically.

Current research suggests that humans don't remember every detail of an experience. A complex experience appears to be reduced to what might be described as a memory *marker*. It appears that when a human remembers, s/he retrieves a marker from the subconscious stratum and "dreams" up the original stimuli. This process provides an explanation of the adage: "Put two people in the same room in the same situation and you'll get two different stories about what happened."

On the other hand, the programmer has total control over which portions of a program's experience will be transferred to the program subconscious memory stratum. With that control comes the difficult task of determining which data will be lost during the reduction process of converting the program's experience (held as data) into a marker. The performance of the program will in part be determined by the cleverness of the algorithm used in this process. Designing that algorithm can be very challenging.

Note that we have drawn from *Webster's New World Dictionary of the American Language* in defining the following terms: objective artificial intelligence, program instinct, program learning, and program consciousness. Understanding the meaning of these terms will prove key in both understanding and applying the OAI paradigm.

1.4 Objective artificial intelligence

objective *adj.* 1. existing as an object or fact, independent of the mind; real....

artificial *adj.* 1. made by human work...; not natural....

intelligence *n.* 1. the ability to learn or understand....

We selected the term *objective artificial intelligence* to support the notion that a program produced by humans may be coded to demonstrate learning and to respond like a human. That means it can be coded to evaluate data in a humanlike fashion and can demonstrate the capability of adaptive behavior change in a designated environment by learning from its experiences.

It seems appropriate at this time to state that we believe the learning algorithms residing in the domain of a computer program to be unique to the fundamental nature of that program. Using the OAI paradigm will provide a program designer with a framework within which to develop algorithms that facilitate learning. Ultimately, however, the development of algorithms which facilitate learning will rise and fall on the strength of the program designer's creative and intellectual resources.

The results of using the OAI paradigm during the program development cycles should not be viewed in an all-or-nothing way. Rather, it would be more constructive to conceive of the results in the following way: it may be said that the degree to which a program successfully implements OAI design methodology is the degree to which humanlike response and learning will take place.

Program instinct

instinct *n.* 1. inborn tendency to behave in a way characteristic of that species.

We define *program instinct* as an innate tendency to respond to data input to the program with behaviors appropriate to the program environment, before any adaptation or learning has taken place. Most traditional computer programs rely solely on program instinct to make decisions. Program instinct is hardcoded into the program at compile and link time. Building program instinct into a program can give it the look and feel of a humanlike response from the get-go. As humanlike response is idiosyncratic to the program in question, sample humanlike responses are presented throughout the examples described in this book.

Program learning

learning *n.* 1. the acquiring of knowledge or a skill.

Program learning refers to a program's ability to alter its behavior in an adaptive fashion via the process of acquiring new knowledge or skills. Program learning draws from data which have been created during program execution, analyzed, and then transferred to the program subconscious. Program learning takes place during the program's execution process by examining the results of this data analysis and subsequently altering the course of its behavior in an adaptive direction.

Program consciousness

consciousness *n.* 1.... 2. the totality of one's thoughts and feelings.

Program consciousness refers to all the memory used when managing data. Both RAM and disk memory are used. Using program consciousness proves key to implementing the OAI paradigm, because memory plays a pivotal role in learning.

1.5 OAI suitability query

This section presents guidelines which you might find helpful in determining if a programming project is a good candidate for being designed using the OAI paradigm. Although we (and some of the manuscript's reviewers) have found using these guidelines useful as starting points for developing learning algorithms, they may tickle your fancy and they may not. Different strokes....

The first step of this process is to decide if your existing project or future programming project will benefit from being designed using the OAI paradigm. The decision should not be judged in a yes/no framework. You might decide that your program is a weak, moderate, or strong candidate based on your evaluation. Think in gradations. The OAI suitability queries are:

- Is there any aspect of the program which will benefit from humanlike performance?
- What do you want your program to learn?
- What is the nature of the demonstrated learning's quantifiable results?

Is there any benefit from demonstrating humanlike performance?

Answering this question takes you to the heart of the first performance boost claimed by the OAI paradigm. If your program needs to crunch data, you'd want it to function more like a computer than a human. Computers are very strong at manipulating data. Humans are not. If your programming project is, say, a game, then developing a humanlike response can make it better.

What do you want the program to learn?

Answering this question takes you to the heart of the second performance boost claimed by the OAI paradigm. If a program can clearly demonstrate that it can learn, the fundamental character of its performance can be vastly improved. For example, in the early stages of Drop Four's development, program instinct could take game play only so far. Once a beta tester found a winning sequence of moves, her/his interest in playing the game rapidly waned: "Hey, I can beat the game every time. It's not fun to play anymore!"

As soon as the early learning algorithms were implemented in Drop Four, beta testers kept coming back again and again. In fact, during an early test trial of the simplest learning methodology, a beta tester hammered the keyboard hard when Dr. Plopper foiled his favorite sequence of moves the second time he tried them. That moment during the beta trials said more about the power of learning than anything we could write.

What is the nature of the demonstrated learning's quantifiable results?

If you answered the first two questions in a generally positive fashion, taking a look at the properties of the learning will give you a sense of whether using the OAI program development methodology will be worth your time. For example, if your program predicts the results of a horse race and can increase its correct prediction rate from 45% to 48% after be being redesigned using OAI methodology, will it prove worth your while? Will it increase sales? What would happen, however, if the correct prediction rate rose from 45%, say, to 55%? 60%? 75%?

I'm sure you get our point. Choosing to use the OAI paradigm in the program design process is a decision that you make based on whether you feel the program's performance boosts of a humanlike response and learning from experience will prove significant.

What does proving significance imply? Should a program be redesigned to boost its performance if that won't increase program sales or user productivity by an order of magnitude? These are subjective questions, and must be explored before deciding to adopt the OAI paradigm for a new or redesigned program.

1.6 OAI implementation overview

We suggest that you begin using the OAI paradigm by stating the programming problem which you wish to solve. A good place to start when developing the problem statement is by reviewing the results of the OAI suitability guidelines exercise. Your answers concerning "What do you want the program to learn?" and "Is there any aspect of the program which will benefit from humanlike performance?" will prove eminently useful. Once you feel comfortable with your problem statement it will be time to begin the analysis and design stages.

At first glance, it makes great sense that one would assume that the OAI problem statement, analysis, design, and implementation might flow in a linear fashion. For example:

- State the problem.
- Analyze the problem.
- Design a solution to the problem.
- Implement the solution to the problem.

Our practical experience with OAI methodology has taught us that in reality an OAI methodology sequence would probably look more like this:

State the problem
DO
    DO
        Analyze the problem
    WHILE   *Analysis doesn't seem best*
    DO
        Design a solution
    WHILE   *Design doesn't seem best*
    Implement the solution
WHILE   *Implementation doesn't effectively solve problem*

Note that we suggest you return to the analysis process if you're not satisfied with the implementation. This recommendation is based on our experience. Although we often struggle very hard in analyzing a problem, rarely do we come up with the best analysis the first time. If we developed a design from a weak analysis, the code implementation never seemed to provide the most effective problem solution. Was the ineffective program solution caused by a weak design or by a solid design of a weak analysis? Since the OAI paradigm dictates that the analysis precede the design, and the design precede the implementation, if the implementation is a weak solution to the problem, it's logical to return to the problem analysis process.

At this juncture it would be proper for you to ask, "How can one determine if the initial program implementation provides the best solution to the problem?" We suspect that you most likely will not know the answer to that question for sure. At such a moment, it would seem proper to review the project timeline milestones to determine if there's time to continue developing a more powerful implementation. Ah, practical matters.

Problem statement

In general, your OAI problem statement should state the performance specifications for the program in question and inquire as to whether using the OAI paradigm will enhance program performance. Stating the problem in this way will provide a nice focus for the initial analysis and design processes. An example of a problem statement might be:

1.6 OAI IMPLEMENTATION OVERVIEW

Can a chess program starting at some initial, simple level be improved by using OAI analysis and design methodology?

OAI analysis

The OAI analysis process can be viewed as a search for information which proceeds via an examination of all data which prove directly related to program execution. This search for information can be thought of as a process in which you make a questioning observation about the information derived from the data and follow with an answer. That answer then becomes the starting point for the generation of another question. Although more than one question might come to mind, we encourage you to follow this branch of inquiry to its logical conclusion. At that point you should repeat the process until all branches of your analysis have been fully explored. In essence, this can be though of as a data decomposition process. OAI analysis centers on culling all potential information which may be drawn from the data. No data should on first glance be considered trivial.

For example, in a computer game having two players we can keep track of each player's moves. What information can we draw from the game's move list? We can construct the location of pieces on the game board after each move. What information can be drawn from the game board positions? The quality of the players' positions. What conclusion can be drawn from the quality of the position for one player or the other? There is a relationship between a player's moves and the quality of that player's position on the board. And so on.

OAI design

OAI design can be thought of as the development of strategies which point toward ways to add learning and humanlike responses to a program's performance. The basis of developing these strategies will be grounded in the fertile ground of the analysis.

For example, let's start by presenting and then expanding slightly upon the previously stated analysis. In a computer game having two players we can keep track of each player's moves. What information can we draw from the game's move list? We can construct the location of pieces on the game board after each move. What information can be drawn from the game board positions? The quality of the players' positions. What can be inferred from the quality of player's position? There is a relationship between a player's moves and the quality of that player's position on the board. If there is a relationship between a move and the pursuant quality of the game board for the player that made that move then, hey, we may be able to find a better move. Can we find a better move and demonstrate learning?

The design begins. Let's turn to the question, "How can we find a move to prevent a poor position from occurring?" The answer is to __. Finding an answer to your question begins the design process.

1.7 Summary

Using the objective artificial intelligence paradigm during the program development process leads to a program which possesses the following qualities:

- Demonstrates learning from its experiences
- Behaves in a humanlike fashion.

The program consciousness is seen as being composed of RAM and disk memory. The program operates on data residing in the program consciousness. The top memory stratum of the program consciousness model is called the *program conscious* stratum. This memory holds the data which are currently being processed. The second stratum is called *program subconscious*. This stratum is composed of markers (data which have been reduced from their original state). These markers have been created and stored by the program. The data markers in the program subconscious prove crucial in the implementation of OAI-based algorithms.

The OAI suitability, query, problem statement, analysis, and design process may help facilitate your development of programs which will learn from their experiences and respond as a human might.

chapter 2

Case study—Tic Tac Toe

We have chosen Tic Tac Toe as a demo OAI program for several reasons. First, it is a game and program with which most people are familiar. Second, it is much simpler than the second case study considered in this book. However, it does allow us to highlight some very important points.

The first version of Tic Tac Toe uses what we call the *forced move algorithm* to implement learning. Details of the forced move algorithm follow later in the book. This proves to be only a partial solution to the problem: under certain circumstances, the computer's second move proves critical in determining if a tie can be obtained, and the forced move algorithm fails to produce learning for the second computer move.

The second demonstration program rectifies the failure of the forced move algorithm by adding program instinct to ensure that the proper second move will always be played. This addition is trivial.

The third demonstration program rectifies the failure of the forced move algorithm to demonstrate learning on the second move by using a different learning algorithm. We call this the *move elimination algorithm*. The move elimination algorithm will be fully explained in Section 2.5.

The contrast between the enhancement of program instinct in version 2 and the enhancement of learning through the use of the move elimination algorithm is of interest. In this case, the enhancement of program instinct proves trivial and the design and implementation of the move elimination algorithm are not. We believe that in the case of Tic Tac Toe, a real-world solution would be to enhance program instinct.

Simple. Quick. Effective. Fast to code. The learning proffered by the move elimination algorithm is, of course, juicier but dicey coding, and certainly not worth the time in a real-world situation.

Let's continue by looking at the OAI suitability query, analysis, and design phases.

2.1 Suitability query

Is there any aspect of the program which will benefit from humanlike response?

Yes. Although Tic Tac Toe can be programmed without OAI, for our purposes, the moves that the computer makes will benefit by using humanlike learning.

Given that our program will always play second in the game, what do you want the computer to learn?

We want it to start from some basic level, and learn from its losses so that it reaches the point where it doesn't lose.

What is the nature of the demonstrated learning's quantifiable results?

The result of the learning will simply be the result of the games against a human player—a win, a loss, or a draw.

2.2 OAI implementation overview of Tic Tac Toe

Problem statement

Can a Tic Tac Toe program starting at some initial, simple level be improved by using OAI analysis and design methodology?

Analysis

In this case, there are two directions that the question and answer format of the analyses may take. The directions may be said to *branch* every time you get a different answer to the same question. Tic Tac Toe's analysis follows two branching paths.

What type of data does the Tic Tac Toe program have? (*Note:* a branch is possible here.) The players in the game produce a record of moves. What can we do with the move list? We can determine if the computer move has been forced (meaning it has blocked a win for the human). What can we do with the forced move information?

Analysis discussion

The simplest process for the computer to base its moves upon is a random one, so we will start with that as our basic level. Obviously, the computer at this point will lose almost every game. We could design it so that it learns to block losses, but that is simple enough to build right into the program as program instinct.

Before we continue this discussion we need to present the game board notation:

0	1	2
3	4	5
6	7	8

Design

What type of data does the Tic Tac Toe program have? The players in a the game produce a record of moves. What can we do with the move list? We can determine if the computer move has been forced (meaning it has blocked a win for the human). What can we do with the forced move information? We can trace back from the last move that the computer has made (which we know will be forced) and seek to find a move which could alter the loss sequence.

Design discussion

At this point, the computer can block losses, but it still loses to combinations that set up two wins on the same move. A sample game is (remember that the human player moves first) 0,1;4,8;3,5;6 wins. The question is how the computer learns from this loss. The answer is the forced move algorithm. We have to decide which move to change and what to change it to if we encounter this game again. Along with each move, we keep track of what kind of move it is—either forced or unforced. In this game, the only forced moves are those that have to block a loss. Then the move to change is the last unforced move, since the game is surely lost after that move. The problem is to decide how to change the move. Since the human player's next move sets up the combination, we will replace our move with the human player's next move. Now we need some way of remembering our analysis. We will store the records in the program subconscious. Each record consists of the move to be changed, the move that is to be substituted, and the list of moves from the game. In our example, the last unforced move is the second one (represented by 1, since the first move is 0), and the replacement move is 4. So the record would look like 1-4-0-1-4-8-3-5-6. Now in future games, when the computer has to move, we can examine the records to see if the game has been played before. First, we make sure that the record shows that this particular move needs to be changed, and then we compare the list of moves up to this point to the list in the record. If they are the same, then we make the substitute move included in the record. Finally then, we must read and write this memory buffer to a file before and after the game. Also we keep track of the number of saved records, and read and write that to the same file.

2.3 Tic Tac Toe version 1

Listing 2.1 presents the source code to ttt.h, the header file for version 1 of Tic Tac Toe. Listing 2.2 presents the source code to ttt.c, the first version of Tic Tac Toe. This program implements forced move learning.

❑ **Listing 2.1**   Source code for version 1 of Tic Tac Toe.

```
///////////////////////////////////
//
// TTT.H
//
// Tic Tac Toe header file.
//

#define EMPTY          0
#define X              1
#define O              2
#define DRAW           3

#define FALSE          0
#define TRUE           1
```

2.3 TIC TAC TOE VERSION 1

```c
#define HUMAN        0
#define COMP         1

#define NO_MOVE      10

#define FORCED       1
#define UNFORCED     0

#define OFFSET       11
#define GAMES        100
#define MEM_SIZE     (GAMES * OFFSET)

typedef int board_t[3][3];

int game_over(board_t board, int turn);
void print_board(board_t board);
void copy_board(board_t board1, board_t board2);
int get_human_move(board_t board);
void make_move(board_t board, int move, int turn);
void print_message(int player);
int get_comp_move(board_t board,
                  int turn, int counter,
                  int move_type[9],
                  int memory[MEM_SIZE],
                  int moves[9],
                  int mem_count);
int random_move(board_t board);
int check_loss(board_t board, int turn);
void analyze_loss(int moves[9],
                  int move_type[9],
                  int memory[MEM_SIZE],
                  int counter,
                  int *mem_count);
void add_loss(int memory[MEM_SIZE],
              int *mem_count,
              int move,
              int change,
              int moves[9]);
int old_loss_check(int counter,
                   int memory[MEM_SIZE],
                   int moves[9],
                   int mem_count);
void open_data_base(int memory[MEM_SIZE],
                    int *mem_count);
```

```c
void close_data_base(int memory[MEM_SIZE],
                     int *mem_count); ■
```

❏ **Listing 2.2** Source code for version 1 of ttt.c.

```c
///////////////////////////////////
//
// TTT.C
//
// Tic Tac Toe demo program.
//

#include <stdio.h>
#include <stdlib.h>
#include <time.h>
#include <fcntl.h>
#include <sys\stat.h>
#include "ttt.h"

////////////////////////////////////////////////
// game_over checks if a given player
// has three in a row on a given board.
// It returns either TRUE or FALSE.
//

int game_over(board_t board, int turn)
{
int i, j;

    for (i= 0; i < 3; i++) {
        if ((board[i][0] == turn) &&
            (board[i][1] == turn) &&
            (board[i][2] == turn)) {
          return TRUE;
          }
        if ((board[0][i] == turn) &&
            (board[1][i] == turn) &&
            (board[2][i] == turn)) {
          return TRUE;
          }
      }
```

2.3 TIC TAC TOE VERSION 1

```
    if ((board[0][0] == turn) &&
        (board[1][1] == turn) &&
        (board[2][2] == turn)) {
      return TRUE;
      }
    if ((board[2][0] == turn) &&
        (board[1][1] == turn) &&
        (board[0][2] == turn)) {
      return TRUE;
      }

    return FALSE;

}

////////////////////////////////////////////////
// print_board prints out a given board
// using X's, O's, and numbers to
// represent the nine different positions
// on the board.
//

void print_board(board_t board)
{
int i, j;

    for (i= 0; i < 3; i++) {
       printf("\n");
       for (j= 0; j < 3; j++) {
          if (board[i][j] == X) {
             printf(" X ");
             }
          else if (board[i][j] == O) {
             printf(" O ");
             }
          else {
             printf(" %d ", (3*i+j) );
             }
          }
       }

    printf("\n");

}
```

```c
///////////////////////////////////////////////
// copy_board copies the first
// board to the second.
//

void copy_board(board_t board1, board_t board2)
{
int i, j;

    for (i= 0; i < 3; i++) {
       for (j= 0; j < 3; j++) {
          board2[i][j]= board1[i][j];
          }
       }

}

///////////////////////////////////////////////
// get_human_move prompts the player and accepts
// a number from 0-8 that represents a square
// on the board.  It repeats the prompt until
// a legal move is entered.
//

int get_human_move(board_t board)
{
int move;

    do {
       printf("\nenter move (0-8) : ");
       scanf("%d", &move);
       if (board[move / 3][move % 3] == EMPTY) {
          break;
          }
       } while (TRUE);

    return move;

}
```

2.3 TIC TAC TOE VERSION 1

```c
//////////////////////////////////////////////
// get_human_move prompts the player and accepts
// a number from 0-8 that represents a square
// on the board.  It repeats the prompt until
// a legal move is entered.
//

void make_move(board_t board, int move, int turn)
{
int row, col;

   row= move / 3;
   col= move % 3;
   board[row][col]= turn;
}

//////////////////////////////////////////////
// print_message prints the appropriate message
// after the game is over.  The winner of the
// game is passed.
//

void print_message(int player)
{

   if (player == HUMAN) {
      printf("\nYou win - I learn\n");
      }
   else if (player == COMP) {
      printf("\nI win - too bad for you\n");
      }
   else {
      printf("\nIt's a draw\n");
      }

}
```

```
/////////////////////////////////////////////////
// get_comp_move makes the computer move using
// different functions such as checking for wins
// and losses, using learning from losses, and
// making a random move as the last resort.
//

int get_comp_move(board_t board,
                  int turn, int counter,
                  int move_type[9],
                  int memory[MEM_SIZE],
                  int moves[9], int mem_count)
{
int move, opponent;

   opponent= (turn == X) ? O : X;

   move= check_loss(board, opponent);
   if (move != NO_MOVE) {
      move_type[counter]= FORCED;
      return move;
      }

   move= check_loss(board, turn);
   if (move != NO_MOVE) {
      move_type[counter]= FORCED;
      return move;
      }

   move= old_loss_check(counter, memory, moves, mem_count);
   if (move != NO_MOVE) {
      move_type[counter]= UNFORCED;
      return move;
      }

   move_type[counter]= UNFORCED;
   return (random_move(board));

}
```

2.3 TIC TAC TOE VERSION 1

```
////////////////////////////////////////////////
// check_loss looks to see if the passed player
// has to block a loss.  It uses an extra board
// to simulate moves and then checks to see if
// the opponent has won.
//

int check_loss(board_t board, int turn)
{
board_t board2;
int i, opponent;

   opponent= (turn == X) ? O : X;

   for (i= 0; i < 9; i++) {
      copy_board(board, board2);
      if (board2[i / 3][ i % 3] == EMPTY) {
         make_move(board2, i, opponent);
         if (game_over(board2, opponent)) {
            return i;
            }
         }
      }

   return NO_MOVE;

}


////////////////////////////////////////////////
// random_move makes a random move.
//

int random_move(board_t board)
{
int move;

   while (TRUE) {
      randomize();
      move= random(1000) % 9;
      if (board[move / 3][move % 3] == EMPTY) {
         return move;
         }
      }
}
```

//
// analyze_loss examines the record of the moves
// and types of moves of a lost game. It then
// uses the forced move algorithm to find the
// move to change and how to change it.

```c
void analyze_loss(int moves[9],
                  int move_type[9],
                  int memory[MEM_SIZE],
                  int counter,
                  int *mem_count)
{
int move, change;

    move= counter - 2;

    while (move_type[move]==FORCED) {
       move -= 2;
       }

    change= moves[move+1];

    add_loss(memory, mem_count, move, change, moves);
}
```

//
// add_loss saves a record of the game in the
// proper format into the memory buffer if there
// is enough room.
//

```c
void add_loss(int memory[MEM_SIZE],
              int *mem_count,
              int move,
              int change,
              int moves[9])
{
int *begin, i;

    if (*mem_count == GAMES) {
       return;
       }
```

2.3 TIC TAC TOE VERSION 1

```
      begin= (memory + (*mem_count * OFFSET));

      *begin++= move;

      *begin++= change;

      for (i= 0; i < 9; i++) {
         *begin++= moves[i];
         }

      ++(*mem_count);
}

//////////////////////////////////////////////////
// old_loss_check uses the memory buffer to see
// if the sequence of moves has been played before
// and returns the correct move if so.
//

int old_loss_check(int counter,
                   int memory[MEM_SIZE],
                   int moves[9],
                   int mem_count)
{
int i, j, found;
int move;

   for(i= mem_count-1; i >= 0; i--) {
      if (memory[(i*OFFSET)]==counter) {
         found= 1;
         for(j= 0; j < counter ; j++) {
            if (moves[j] != memory[(i*OFFSET) + j + 2]) {
               found= 0;
               break;
               }
            }
         if (found) {
            move= memory[(i*OFFSET) + 1];
            return move;
            }
         }
      }
   return NO_MOVE;
}
```

```c
//////////////////////////////////////////////
// open_data_base reads in the memory buffer,
// record counter, and second_move array from
// the file "memory.dat".  If the file
// doesn't exist, all arrays are initialized.
//

void open_data_base(int memory[MEM_SIZE], int *mem_count)
{
int handle;

    handle= open("memory.dat", O_CREAT |
                               O_TRUNC |
                               O_BINARY, S_IREAD |
                               S_IWRITE);
    if(handle == -1) {
       *mem_count= 0;
       memset(memory, MEM_SIZE, 0);
       return;
       }

    if(read(handle, mem_count, 2) == -1) {
       printf("\n read error \n");
       }

    if(read(handle, memory, MEM_SIZE) == -1) {
       printf("\n read error \n");
       }

    close(handle);
}

//////////////////////////////////////////////
// close_data_base writes the memory buffer,
// record counter, and second_move array to
// the file "memory.dat".
//

void close_data_base(int memory[MEM_SIZE], int *mem_count)
{
int handle;
```

2.3 TIC TAC TOE VERSION 1

```
      remove("memory.dat");
      handle= open("memory.dat", O_CREAT |
                                 O_TRUNC |
                                 O_BINARY,
                                 S_IREAD |
                                 S_IWRITE);
      if(handle == -1) {
         printf("\nerror opening file\n");
         exit(1);
      }

      if(write(handle, mem_count, 2) == -1) {
         printf("\n write error \n");
      }

      if(write(handle, memory, MEM_SIZE) == -1) {
         printf("\n write error \n");
      }

      close(handle);
   }

   void main()
   {
   board_t board= {{EMPTY, EMPTY, EMPTY},
                   {EMPTY, EMPTY, EMPTY},
                   {EMPTY, EMPTY, EMPTY}};
   int turn= X;
   int player= HUMAN;
   int move;
   int counter;
   int moves[9];
   int move_type[9];
   int memory[MEM_SIZE];
   int mem_count= 0;

      open_data_base(memory, &mem_count);

      counter= 0;

      while (TRUE) {

         print_board(board);
```

```
      if (player == HUMAN) {
         move= get_human_move(board);
         move_type[counter]= 0;
         }
      else {
         move= get_comp_move(board,
                             turn,
                             counter,
                             move_type,
                             memory,
                             moves,
                             mem_count);
         }

      make_move(board, move, turn);
      moves[counter]= move;
      ++counter;

      if (game_over(board, turn)) {
         print_board(board);
         print_message(player);
         if (player == HUMAN) {
            analyze_loss(moves,
                         move_type,
                         memory,
                         counter,
                         &mem_count);
            }
         break;
         }

      if (counter == 9) {
         print_board(board);
         print_message(DRAW);
         break;
         }

      player= (player == HUMAN) ? COMP : HUMAN;
      turn= (turn == X) ? O : X;

      }

   close_data_base(memory, &mem_count);
} ■
```

2.4 Tic Tac Toe version 2

After playing with the game at this level, we see that the forced move learning works in some situations, but not in others. It breaks down in games when the second move must be changed. This requires further analysis. Now since this is such a simple game, an effective response is easy to build into the program as instinct. We simply decide to move in the center on the second move, or to move in a corner if the center is already occupied.

Version 2 of the Tic Tac Toe program uses enhanced program instinct to correct the failure of the forced move algorithm to provide learning for the second move of the game. The code which implements the bolstered program instinct proves to be trivial.

Since the difference between versions 1 and 2 are minimal, we'll present only the code which is either new or modified. An additional function prototype has been added to the ttt.h file. It is presented in Listing 2.3.

❑ **Listing 2.3** Function prototype added to version 2 of ttt.h.

```
/////////////////////////////////
//
// TTT.H
//
// Tic Tac Toe header file.
//
.
.
.
int second_move(board_t board);
.
.
.  ■
```

Listing 2.4 presents the source code to those functions which have either had source modified or have not been included in version 1 of ttt.c (Listing 2.2).

❏ **Listing 2.4** Source code to version 2 of ttt.c.

```
///////////////////////////////////
//
// TTT.C
//
// Tic Tac Toe demo program.
//
 .
 .
 .
int get_comp_move(board_t board,
                  int turn,
                  int counter,
                  int move_type[9],
                  int memory[MEM_SIZE],
                  int moves[9],
                  int mem_count)
{
int move, opponent;

   opponent= (turn == X) ? O : X;

   // second_move(...) function called here.

   if (counter == 1) {
      move= second_move(board);
      move_type[counter]= UNFORCED;
      return move;
      }

   move= check_loss(board, opponent);
   if (move != NO_MOVE) {
      move_type[counter]= FORCED;
      return move;
      }

   move= check_loss(board, turn);
   if (move != NO_MOVE) {
      move_type[counter]= FORCED;
      return move;
      }
```

```
      move= old_loss_check(counter, memory, moves, mem_count);
      if (move != NO_MOVE) {
         move_type[counter]= UNFORCED;
         return move;
         }

      move_type[counter]= UNFORCED;
      return (random_move(board));

}

// Program instinct takes care of
// making the second move of the
// game. The program instinct
// solution to the second move
// problem proves simple and
// effective.

int second_move(board_t board)
{

   if (board[1][1] == EMPTY) {
      return 4;
      }
   else {
      return 0;
      }
} ∎
```

2.5 Tic Tac Toe version 3

We see that version 2 is a very strong program. Instead of relying on program instinct to make the second move, we can design a new type of learning. Our analysis has provided insight indicating that instead of directly trying to find the correct move, we should learn which moves are wrong. We call this learning-based algorithm the *move elimination*, because the wrong moves are eliminated from the list of possible moves.

   This learning is used if the forced move function finds that the second move is the key move. What we do then is use a 9×9 array to the keep track of all possible first and second moves. After a loss then, we say that a particular two-move combination should not be used again. In future games, we make a random second move, as long as it has not been flagged as a losing move. We save this second-move array in the same way, as a memory buffer.

Version 3 provides an alternative solution to the second move problem, which had been previously solved using program instinct. Devising a learning algorithm to take care of this special case proved more difficult to program than the program instinct–based solution. For this reason, the source code to the third version of the Tic Tac Toe program is heavily commented.

Note also that the robustness of the forced-move can be improved by taking advantage of symmetry and creating more than one record from a loss.

Listing 2.5 presents the source code to the version 3 ttt.h header file, and Listing 2.6 presents the source code to the version 3 ttt.c.

❏ **Listing 2.5** Source code to version 3 of Tic Tac Toe.

```
/////////////////////////////////
//
// TTT.H
//
// Tic Tac Toe header file.
//

// Constant definitions.
#define EMPTY           0
#define X               1
#define O               2
#define DRAW            3

#define FALSE           0
#define TRUE            1

#define HUMAN           0
#define COMP            1

#define NO_MOVE         10

#define FORCED          1
#define UNFORCED        0

#define OFFSET          11
#define GAMES           100
#define MEM_SIZE        (GAMES * OFFSET)
```

2.5 TIC TAC TOE VERSION 3

```
#define NOT_ALLOWED    1
#define ALLOWED        0

// Special type definitions.
typedef int board_t[3][3];

// Function prototypes.
int game_over(board_t board, int turn);
void print_board(board_t board);
void copy_board(board_t board1, board_t board2);
int get_human_move(board_t board);
void make_move(board_t board, int move, int turn);
void print_message(int player);
int get_comp_move(board_t board,
                  int turn,
                  int counter,
                  int move_type[9],
                  int memory[MEM_SIZE],
                  int moves[9],
                  int mem_count,
                  int second_moves[9][9]);
int random_move(board_t board);
int check_loss(board_t board, int turn);
void analyze_loss(int moves[9],
                  int move_type[9],
                  int memory[MEM_SIZE],
                  int counter,
                  int *mem_count,
                  int second_moves[9][9]);
void add_loss(int memory[MEM_SIZE],
              int *mem_count,
              int move,
              int change,
              int moves[9]);
int old_loss_check(int counter,
                   int memory[MEM_SIZE],
                   int moves[9],
                   int mem_count);
void open_data_base(int memory[MEM_SIZE],
                    int *mem_count,
                    int second_moves[9][9]);
void close_data_base(int memory[MEM_SIZE],
                     int *mem_count,
                     int second_moves[9][9]);
```

```c
void analyze_second(int moves[9],
                    int second_moves[9][9]);
int learned_second_move(board_t board,
                        int moves[9],
                        int second_moves[9][9]); ■
```

❑ **Listing 2.6** Source code to version 3 of ttt.c.

```c
/////////////////////////////////
//
// TTT.C
//
// Tic Tac Toe demo program.
//

#include <stdio.h>
#include <stdlib.h>
#include <time.h>
#include <fcntl.h>
#include <sys\stat.h>
#include <mem.h>
#include <io.h>
#include "ttt.h"


///////////////////////////////////////////////
// game_over checks if a given player
// has three in a row on a given board.
// It returns either TRUE or FALSE.
//

int game_over(board_t board, int turn)
{
int i, j;      // loop variables

   for (i= 0; i < 3; i++) {

      // Examine all three rows.
      if ((board[i][0] == turn) &&
          (board[i][1] == turn) &&
          (board[i][2] == turn)) {
         return TRUE;
         }
```

2.5 TIC TAC TOE VERSION 3

```c
      // Examine all three columns.
      if ((board[0][i] == turn) &&
          (board[1][i] == turn) &&
          (board[2][i] == turn)) {
        return TRUE;
        }
      }

   // Examine both diagonals.
   if ((board[0][0] == turn) &&
       (board[1][1] == turn) &&
       (board[2][2] == turn)) {
     return TRUE;
     }
   if ((board[2][0] == turn) &&
       (board[1][1] == turn) &&
       (board[0][2] == turn)) {
     return TRUE;
     }

   // No wins for the player.
   return FALSE;
}

////////////////////////////////////////////////
// print_board prints out a given board
// using X's, O's, and numbers to
// represent the nine different positions
// on the board.
//

void print_board(board_t board)
{
int i, j;     // loop variables

   for (i= 0; i < 3; i++) {
      printf("\n");
      for (j= 0; j < 3; j++) {

         // For each square, print piece if occupied.
         // Otherwise, print corresponding number.
         if (board[i][j] == X) {
            printf(" X ");
            }
```

```
            else if (board[i][j] == O) {
               printf(" O ");
               }
            else {
               printf(" %d ", (3*i+j) );
               }
            }
         }

    printf("\n");
}

//////////////////////////////////////////////////
// copy_board copies the first
// board to the second.
//

void copy_board(board_t board1, board_t board2)
{
int i, j;      // loop variables

    for (i= 0; i < 3; i++) {
       for (j= 0; j < 3; j++) {
          board2[i][j]= board1[i][j];
          }
       }

}

//////////////////////////////////////////////////
// get_human_move prompts the player and accepts
// a number from 0-8 that represents a square
// on the board.  It repeats the prompt until
// a legal move is entered.
//

int get_human_move(board_t board)
{
int move;

    do {

       // Prompt player.
       printf("\nenter move (0-8) : ");
```

2.5 TIC TAC TOE VERSION 3

```c
         // Get player's move.
         scanf("%d", &move);

         // Return if legal move (square is empty).
         if (board[move / 3][move % 3] == EMPTY) {
            break;
            }
         } while (TRUE);

   return move;
}

/////////////////////////////////////////////////
// make_move takes a number from 0-8 and
// puts a given piece in the corresponding place
// on the given board.
//

void make_move(board_t board, int move, int turn)
{
int row, col;
   row= move / 3;
   col= move % 3;
   board[row][col]= turn;
}

/////////////////////////////////////////////////
// print_message prints the appropriate message
// after the game is over.  The winner of the
// game is passed.
//

void print_message(int player)
{
   if (player == HUMAN) {
      printf("\nYou win - I learn\n");
      }
   else if (player == COMP) {
      printf("\nI win - sucks for you\n");
      }
   else {
      printf("\nIt's a draw\n");
      }
}
```

```
//////////////////////////////////////////////
// get_comp_move makes the computer move using
// different functions, such as checking for wins
// and losses, using learning from losses, and
// making a random move as the last resort.
//
int get_comp_move(board_t board,
                  int turn,
                  int counter, int move_type[9],
                  int memory[MEM_SIZE],
                  int moves[9],
                  int mem_count,
                  int second_moves[9][9])
{
int move, opponent;
   opponent= (turn == X) ? O : X;

   // Use learning on the second move.
   if (counter == 1) {
      move= learned_second_move(board, moves, second_moves);
      move_type[counter]= UNFORCED;
      return move;
      }

   // Make move for win if possible.
   move= check_loss(board, opponent);
   if (move != NO_MOVE) {
      move_type[counter]= FORCED;
      return move;
      }

   // Make move to block loss if needed.
   move= check_loss(board, turn);
   if (move != NO_MOVE) {
      move_type[counter]= FORCED;
      return move;
      }

   // Make move based on previous loss.
   move= old_loss_check(counter, memory, moves, mem_count);
   if (move != NO_MOVE) {
      move_type[counter]= UNFORCED;
      return move;
      }
```

2.5 TIC TAC TOE VERSION 3

```c
   // Make random move as last resort.
   move_type[counter]= UNFORCED;
   return (random_move(board));
}

/////////////////////////////////////////////////
// check_loss looks to see if the passed player
// has to block a loss.  It uses an extra board
// to simulate moves and then checks to see if
// the opponent has won.
//

int check_loss(board_t board, int turn)
{
board_t board2;       // board for simulated moves
int i, opponent;

   opponent= (turn == X) ? O : X;

   // Go through all possible moves.
   for (i= 0; i < 9; i++) {
      copy_board(board, board2);

      // Make move if possible.
      if (board2[i / 3][ i % 3] == EMPTY) {
         make_move(board2, i, opponent);

         // If move produces loss, return it to block.
         if (game_over(board2, opponent)) {
            return i;
            }
         }
      }

   return NO_MOVE;
}

/////////////////////////////////////////////////
// random_move makes a random move.
//

int random_move(board_t board)
{
int move;
```

```
      while (TRUE) {
         randomize();
         move= random(1000) % 9;

         // Return move if legal.
         if (board[move / 3][move % 3] == EMPTY) {
            return move;
            }
         }
}

////////////////////////////////////////////////////
// analyze_loss examines the record of the moves
// and the types of moves of a lost game.  It then
// uses the forced move algorithm to find which
// move to change and which move to make instead.
// In this version, if the move to be changed is
// the second one, then a special function is used
// to apply the second type of learning.
//

void analyze_loss(int moves[9],
                  int move_type[9],
                  int memory[MEM_SIZE],
                  int counter,
                  int *mem_count,
                  int second_moves[9][9])
{
int move, change;

   // Start at computer's last move.
   move= counter - 2;

   // Go to last unforced move.
   while (move_type[move]==FORCED) {
      move -= 2;
      }

   // Use second type of learning if at second move.
   if (move == 1) {
      analyze_second(moves, second_moves);
      return;
      }
```

2.5 TIC TAC TOE VERSION 3

```c
      // New move is player's next move.
      change= moves[move+1];

      // Add record to memory buffer.
      add_loss(memory, mem_count, move, change, moves);
   }

   ///////////////////////////////////////////////
   // add_loss saves a record of the game in the
   // proper format into the memory buffer if there
   // is enough room.
   //

   void add_loss(int memory[MEM_SIZE],
                 int *mem_count, int move,
                 int change, int moves[9])
   {
   int *begin, i;

      // Return immediately if the maximum
      // number of games has already been saved.
      if (*mem_count == GAMES) {
         return;
         }

      // Start at beginning of available buffer.
      begin= (memory + (*mem_count * OFFSET));

      // First save point in game of change.
      *begin++= move;

      // Save move to make instead.
      *begin++= change;

      // Save list of moves of game.
      for (i= 0; i < 9; i++) {
         *begin++= moves[i];
         }

      // Increment counter of records.
      ++(*mem_count);
   }
```

```
///////////////////////////////////////////////
// old_loss_check uses the memory buffer to see
// if the sequence of moves has been played before
// and returns the correct move if it has.
//

int old_loss_check(int counter,
                   int memory[MEM_SIZE],
                   int moves[9],
                   int mem_count)
{
int i, j, found;
int move;

   // Search through all records.
   for(i= mem_count-1; i >= 0; i--) {

      // Proceed only if record specifies change
      // at this particular move.
      if (memory[(i*OFFSET)] == counter) {
         found= 1;

         // Go to next record if moves up to this
         // point are not the same.
         for(j= 0; j < counter ; j++) {

            // Compare each move to moves in the record.
            if (moves[j] != memory[(i*OFFSET) + j + 2]) {
              found= 0;
              break;
              }
            }

         // If record is valid, return saved move.
         if (found) {
           move= memory[(i*OFFSET) + 1];
           return move;
           }
         }
      }

   return NO_MOVE;
}
```

2.5 TIC TAC TOE VERSION 3

```c
//////////////////////////////////////////////
// open_data_base reads in the memory buffer,
// record counter, and second_move array from
// the file "memory.dat" .  If the file
// doesn't exist, all arrays are initialized.
//

void open_data_base(int memory[MEM_SIZE],
                    int *mem_count,
                    int second_moves[9][9])
{
int handle, i;

   // Open memory.dat.
   handle= open("memory.dat", O_CREAT |
                              O_TRUNC |
                              O_BINARY,
                              S_IREAD |
                              S_IWRITE);

   // If file doesn't exist, initialize arrays.
   if(handle == -1) {
      *mem_count= 0;
      memset(memory, MEM_SIZE, 0);
      for (i= 0; i < 9; i++) {

         // All second moves are initially allowed,
         memset(second_moves[i], 9, ALLOWED);

         // but the second move can't be the same as the first.
         second_moves[i][i]= NOT_ALLOWED;
         }
      return;
      }

   // Read in record counter.
   if (read(handle, mem_count, 2) == -1) {
      printf("\n read error \n");
      }

   // Read in memory buffer.
   if (read(handle, memory, MEM_SIZE) == -1) {
      printf("\n read error \n");
      }
```

```c
   // Read in second_moves array.
   for (i= 0; i < 9; i++) {
      if (read(handle, second_moves[i], 9) == -1) {
         printf("\n read error \n");
         }
      }

   // Close file.
   close(handle);
}

////////////////////////////////////////////////////
// close_data_base writes the memory buffer,
// record counter, and second_move array to
// the file "memory.dat".
//

void close_data_base(int memory[MEM_SIZE],
                    int *mem_count,
                    int second_moves[9][9])
{
int handle, i;

   // Erase existing file.
   remove("memory.dat");

   // Open file for writing.
   handle= open("memory.dat", O_CREAT |
                              O_TRUNC |
                              O_BINARY,
                              S_IREAD |
                              S_IWRITE);
   if(handle == -1) {
      printf("\nerror opening file\n");

      // Exit immediately on error.
      exit(1);
      }

   // Write record counter to file.
   if(write(handle, mem_count, 2) == -1) {
      printf("\n write error \n");
      }
```

2.5 TIC TAC TOE VERSION 3

```c
      // Write memory buffer to file.
      if(write(handle, memory, MEM_SIZE) == -1) {
         printf("\n write error \n");
         }

      // Write second_moves array to file.
      for (i= 0; i < 9; i++) {
         if(write(handle, second_moves[i], 9) == -1) {
            printf("\n write error \n");
            }
         }

      // Close file.
      close(handle);
   }

   //////////////////////////////////////////////////
   // analyze_second looks at the list of moves and
   // remembers which move leads to a loss following
   // a certain first move.
   //

   void analyze_second(int moves[9], int second_moves[9][9])
   {

      // Since a loss occured, this second move should
      // not be allowed.
      second_moves[(moves[0])][(moves[1])]= NOT_ALLOWED;


   }


   //////////////////////////////////////////////////
   // learned_second_move uses the second_moves array
   // to make a move that doesn't lead to a loss.
   //

   int learned_second_move(board_t board,
                           int moves[9],
                           int second_moves[9][9])
   {
   int move;

      move= random_move(board);
```

```
      // Get a random move that doesn't lead to a loss.
      while (second_moves[(moves[0])][move] == NOT_ALLOWED) {
         move= random_move(board);
         }
      return move;
   }
void main()
{
board_t board= {{EMPTY, EMPTY, EMPTY},
                {EMPTY, EMPTY, EMPTY},
                {EMPTY, EMPTY, EMPTY}};
int turn= X;
int player= HUMAN;
int move;
int counter;
int moves[9];
int move_type[9];
int memory[MEM_SIZE];
int mem_count= 0;
int second_moves[9][9];

   open_data_base(memory, &mem_count, second_moves);

   counter= 0;

   while (TRUE) {
      print_board(board);

      // Get the next move.
      if (player == HUMAN) {
         move= get_human_move(board);
         move_type[counter]= 0;
         }
      else {
         move= get_comp_move(board,
                             turn,
                             counter,
                             move_type,
                             memory,
                             moves,
                             mem_count,
                             second_moves);
         }
      make_move(board, move, turn);
```

2.5 TIC TAC TOE VERSION 3

```
      // Record move and increment counter.
      moves[counter]= move;
      ++counter;

      if (game_over(board, turn)) {
         print_board(board);
         print_message(player);

         // Learn from loss if computer loses.
         if (player == HUMAN) {
            analyze_loss(moves,
                         move_type,
                         memory,
                         counter,
                         &mem_count,
                         second_moves);
         }

         // End program.
         break;
         }

      // Check if game is a draw.
      if (counter == 9) {
         print_board(board);
         print_message(DRAW);
         break;
         }

      // Switch player and turn.
      player= (player == HUMAN) ? COMP : HUMAN;
      turn= (turn == X) ? O : X;

      }

   close_data_base(memory, &mem_count, second_moves);

} ■
```

2.6 Summary

The Tic Tac Toe demonstration program provides insight into the real-world application of the OAI paradigm. We introduced the idea that the OAI design should decide where program instinct will end and program learning will take over. Where one should begin program learning is clear only when all avenues to bolster program instinct have been taken. Under all other circumstances, when to begin program learning is debatable. The more robust program learning becomes, the less robust program instinct needs to be.

chapter 3

Drop Four case study overview and analysis

Although the nuts and bolts of the learning algorithms used in Drop Four are presented in the remaining portions of the book, we believe that it is important to state at the beginning that the learning-based algorithms used in Drop Four (*forced move* and *three-filled marker disruption*) will be used in a robust fashion. This means that the data created by the original game will be manipulated to create symmetrical sequences and patterns of the original data. The patterns are saved as markers, which are used by the learning algorithms. The markers are used in both offensive and defensive strategies, regardless of the original circumstances surrounding their creation. The markers are also used if Dr. Plopper plays first or second.

That stated, Chapter 3 starts with a detailed look at Drop Four which highlights the effectiveness of using the OAI paradigm in program development. We begin with a brief explanation of four-in-a-row genre games and follow with a descriptive case study which describes the development of Drop Four. This four-in-a-row genre game, played on an 8 × 8 matrix, moves in a humanlike time frame (under 5 seconds on a 486 33-MHz computer) and learns from its losses. This chapter centers on the Drop Four OAI suitability query and analysis.

3.1 Four-in-a-row genre games

The play in four-in-a-row games is quite simple. On a matrix of a given size the players place tiles, stones, or chips starting on one side (usually the bottom) and continuing up toward the other side (usually the top) until one player gets four pieces in a row. The adjacent pieces may be oriented vertically, horizontally, or diagonally. When one player gets four pieces in a row, s/he has won, simple as that.

Traditional four-in-a-row genre games are played on a matrix 7 columns wide by 6 rows high. Figure 3.1 depicts an empty 7×6 matrix.

The game is traditionally played on a vertically oriented board, where players alternate dropping chips down the columns until one player has four chips vertically, horizontally, or diagonally in a row. Figure 3.2 depicts a game-winning pattern in a 7×6 matrix. In this case Black's winning diagonal travels in the SW–NE direction.

In the 7×6 matrix, gaining control of the central column takes on special meaning. If a player gets control of the center column s/he has an increased chance of getting four chips in a row horizontally or diagonally on either side. It's been well established by serious gamesters that if players who move first play perfectly, they will win every time. Case closed.

We, however, chose to expand the traditional game board to an 8×8 matrix. Here the situation becomes dramatically more complex. After evaluating literally hundreds upon hundreds of games played on the 8×8 matrix by players of all abilities, we are

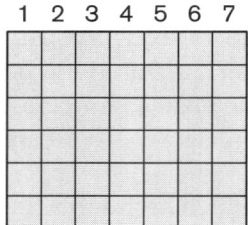

Figure 3.1 7×6 empty matrix.

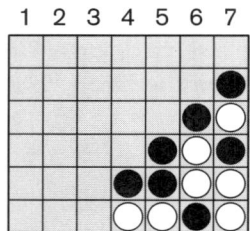

Figure 3.2 Win for Black on a 7×6 matrix.

fairly certain that if there is a forced win for the player who moves first, it must be very deep and take place very late in the ending stages of play. We could not find one. Case still open.

3.2 Drop Four case study

Following our suggestion to anthropomorphize and name the learning portion of the program developed using the OAI paradigm, we named Drop Four's AI persona *Dr. Plopper*. The name was derived from the DOS character animation sequence. When a move was selected by either the human or the computer, an early version of Drop Four was programmed so that a piece would drop down a column and land with a plop. Len is often called *Doc* by his students. You may infer from this sketchy information how Dr. Plopper was formally named.

One other note: when we were applying the OAI paradigm to develop the Drop Four program, the real-world process involved emotional discussions. At times there were virulent disagreements over certain approaches. At other times, we experienced the initial elation of what seemed like a promising analysis, only to crash when a cogent design wouldn't emerge. We have tried to impart the give-and-take tone of our discussions to the analysis, design, and implementation portions of this book. That stated, we begin by running the proposed Drop Four game program through the OAI suitability queries.

3.3 Drop Four's OAI suitability query

Is there any aspect of the program which will benefit from humanlike performance?

When we first began exploring the notion of developing a four-in-a-row genre game program, we took a look at a few public domain implementations written for OS/2 under its Presentation Manager graphical front end. We were shocked to see that moves that would have taken a human under 1 second to make occasionally took as long as 45 seconds on a 486 33-MHz computer. Although 45 seconds is not a long time, it felt like an eternity as we were sitting at the computer terminal waiting for the program to make a move.

At that moment, we realized that adding OAI designed features to reduce the time required to make a decision would increase the level of enjoyment experienced by playing the game, as well as with the efficiency of the program. Our affirmative answer to the first OAI suitability query prompted us to continue.

What do you want your program to learn?

We would like our program to avoid losing two times by the same move sequence.

Game design is a dicey business. If you make the game impossible to beat, then the game will be no fun to play. If you make the game too easy to beat, then it will also be no fun to play. The best compromise would be to make the game's level of difficulty automatically increase as players improve the quality of their game play.

In arcade-style games, that proves to be not as daunting as in strategy games, because the programmer can gradually adjust difficulty parameters as the human player gains skill. For example, in Tetris, the shapes fall a bit faster as you succeed at one level and move on to the next higher one. In a strategy game such as Drop Four, we suspected the ability to increase the game's strength of play by learning from its losses would prove more difficult to implement.

What is the nature of Drop Four's demonstrable learning?

Learning will be demonstrated if the program can avoid a previously experienced loss.

We reasoned that it would be possible for a human player to initially beat Drop Four. The second time that the human would try to beat Drop Four by repeating the move sequence of the previous win, we wanted Drop Four to alter some of its moves to avoid the loss. Now that would be "totally cool!" In addition, we reasoned that it would be sweet if Drop Four could take the wily play that the human had used to previously defeat it and use those techniques against the perpetrator and other human players.

After answering the questions posed by the OAI suitability queries we felt completely convinced that using the OAI paradigm to develop the Drop Four program was the way to go.

3.4 OAI implementation overview of Drop Four

Drop Four problem statement

Can Drop Four's performance be improved by being designed using the OAI paradigm?

3.4 OAI IMPLEMENTATION OVERVIEW OF DROP FOUR

Drop Four analysis (branch 1)

What type of data does the Drop Four program generate? The players produce records of moves. What are moves composed of? They are composed of numbers representing the column where the piece was dropped and whether the move was forced by the human to prevent a loss by Dr. Plopper. What can we do with the move list? We can determine which is Dr. Plopper's last move. What can we do with Dr. Ploppers's last move? We can trace back each move in the list to determine which move would have prevented the loss. How can we find the move which would be the last chance to avoid a forced loss for Dr. Plopper?

Drop Four analysis (branch 2)

What type of data does the Drop Four program generate? The players produce records of moves. What can we do with the move list? We can reconstruct the game board position after each of the moves. What can we do with the game board positions? We can evaluate the relative strength of the players' positions. What are these positions composed of? We can view the game board position as being composed of a series of piece patterns. What can we do with the comparison of the players' move lists and the game board patterns? We can calculate which game board piece patterns will lead to a loss for Dr. Plopper. How can we teach Dr. Plopper to avoid the game board patterns which lead to losses?

Analysis discussion

Branch 1 of Drop Four's analysis led to the development of the forced move algorithm. Details of this algorithm will follow later in the book. Note that since the move list consists of an external event (a human move) and an internal response (a computer-generated move), we believe that any computer program which flows in such a way as to record an externally generated event and respond, then get another externally generated event and respond, etc., is potentially a fine candidate for a variation of the forced move algorithm.

Branch 2 of Drop Four's analysis led to the development of the marker disruption algorithm. Details of this algorithm will follow later in the book. It's appropriate to state that, as with the forced move algorithm, any program which falls into the broad category of recording an event and generating a response and whose data could be viewed in the framework of "patterns" would be potentially a fine candidate for a variation of the marker disruption algorithm.

The Drop Four program will examine the piece locations on the game board and arrive at one of four decisions. These are:

- Dr. Plopper has won.
- Dr. Plopper has lost.
- The game is drawn.
- A move must be generated.

Let's examine each condition. Determining if Dr. Plopper has won the game seems quite simple at first glance. The game board's piece location data can be held by creating a two dimensional 8×8 array. If Dr. Plopper's pieces were assigned one constant value and the human's pieces were assigned another constant value, a routine could be written to ascertain if four of the human's or Dr. Plopper's pieces were in a contiguous position. This takes care of the first two conditions, and certainly seems eminently doable.

Determining if the game is drawn also seems easy. One way would be to determine if an 8-row high column was completely filled with 8 pieces. If that were the case, then attempting to move a piece into that column would be illegal. If all 8 columns of the Drop Four game board were filled with 8 pieces, there would be no legal moves available to Dr. Plopper or the human and the game would be drawn. Another idea might be to determine if each element in the 8×8 array which held the data for the game board were filled with a piece. If all the elements of the data array representing the game board were filled, there would be no legal moves and the game would be drawn.

The last possibility to consider is having Dr. Plopper generate a move. This task is far more complex that the first three. Let's continue at a snail's pace. The move that is generated should have one primary characteristic. It should be made in a timely fashion (in human terms, of course). That's the way that a human would play. From game play experience, it seemed to us that only under the rarest of conditions might a human take more that one minute to decide upon a move. Let's start by analyzing program instinct.

Analyzing Drop Four program instinct

How could we teach Dr. Plopper to make moves in a timely fashion? We decided using program instinct would be a perfect place to start. Although Len is a somewhat skilled chess player, he never really bothered to learn the nuances of four-in-a-row genre games. Narendra, on the other hand, never studied chess but did gain deep expertise at playing four-in-a-row genre games. Since Narendra was deemed the expert, we decided to see how his mind analyzed game positions and selected moves.

3.4 OAI IMPLEMENTATION OVERVIEW OF DROP FOUR

We devised a mock game board, and Len requested that Narendra verbalize all thoughts as he selected his moves. Narendra's verbalizations went something like this:

Move 1 Since there are 8 columns I want to gain some influence in the board's center. That way I'll have winning possibilities in the center and on either side. The purpose is to maximize potential winning possibilities in future game positions.

Moves 2–3 Now I'll try to piece together patterns where three pieces are placed in a position such that the placement of a fourth would result in a win. (We call this a *three-filled* position.)

Moves 4–n First, I'll check to see if I can win the game on the next move. If so, I will make the winning move. If I can't, then I'll see if you can win the game using your next move. If you can, then I'll block your win. If I can't win on the next move and don't need to block you from winning on your next move, I'll continue creating situations where I get three of my pieces aligned so that I may win the game by placing a fourth piece in a four-in-a-row alignment.

The plan, of course, would be to create a game board situation where the opponent would need to block Narendra's win possibility. The move that Narendra's opponent would use to block his win possibility would then set up another win possibility for him. Since Narendra's opponent couldn't move twice in a row, Narendra would make the winning move. In a chess player's parlance, Narendra was using positional considerations (the three-filled pattern) to set up forced combinations. The forced combination was designed so he would win.

To develop a positional vocabulary, we decided to anchor the board orientation vertically (Figure 3.3). In addition, we decided to place traditional compass directions on the board.

In the West–East board direction, there are four possible three-filled possibilities. (Figure 3.4).

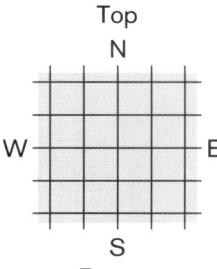

Figure 3.3 Board with compass directions.

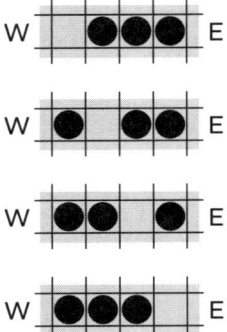

Figure 3.4 West–East three-filled possibilities.

There also might be three-filled winning possibilities in the NW–SE (Figure 3.5) and in the NE–SW directions (Figure 3.6).

Figure 3.7 presents an example of a combination with two three-filled patterns which make up the basis of a forced win combination. If White has the next turn, it must drop a piece into column 5 to block Black's win on the bottom row. White's move fails, however, because once White moves in column 5 Black can follow with a move in column 5 and then win on the SW–NE diagonal. Basically, once this position has been obtained by Black, White is completely lost.

Another tactical winning position might be described as a fork, a ploy familiar to chess players. With a fork, a position is created where the human or computer has two opportunities to win the game occurring at the same time. If it's White's move to

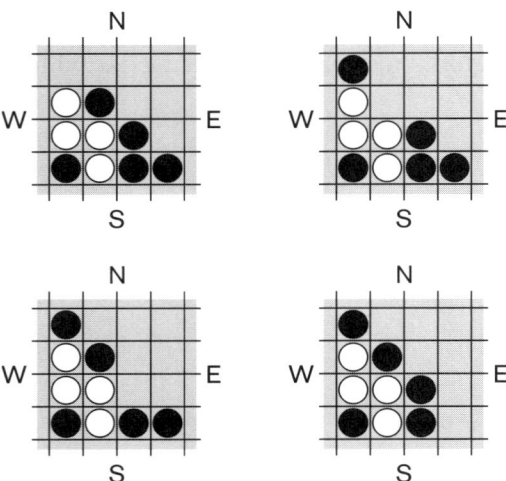

Figure 3.5 NW–SE three-filled possibilities.

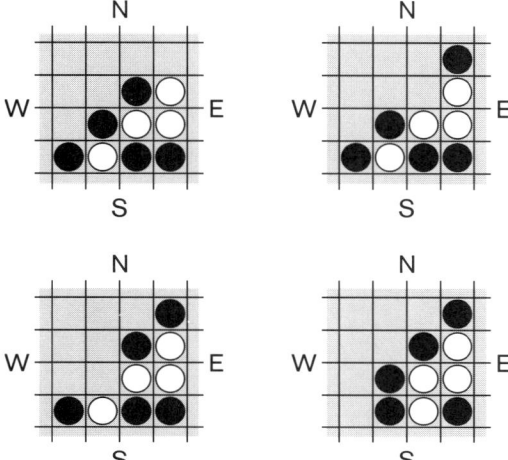

Figure 3.6 NE–SW three-filled possibilities.

make, a play in either column 3 or column 7 will stop both of Black's winning opportunities. Since White is not permitted to make two moves in one turn, Black must win. Figure 3.8 shows a sample game position illustrating a fork.

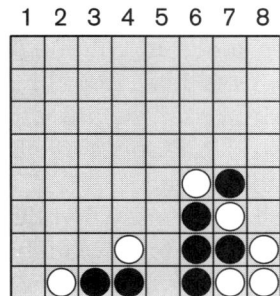

Figure 3.7 Three-filled forced win; White to move and lose.

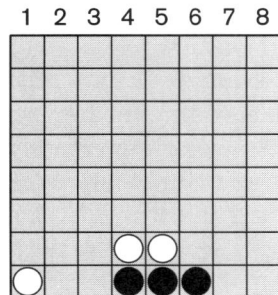

Figure 3.8 A fork; White to move and lose.

Search	Calculation	Evaluations
1-ply	8	8
2-ply	8 × 8	64
3-ply	8 × 8 × 8	512
4-ply	8 × 8 × 8 × 8	4096
5-ply	8 × 8 × 8 × 8 × 8	32,768
6-ply	8 × 8 × 8 × 8 × 8 × 8	262,144

Table 3.1 6-ply search potential position evaluations.

At this point, we realized that we'd need to do a 1-ply search to determine if a possible move would create a new three-filled pattern. The idea was to create a phantom board in the program subconscious, make the 1-ply move, and evaluate the position. At first glance this seemed simple and doable. If there were 8 possible moves for Dr. Plopper to consider, we'd only have to do 8 evaluations of the phantom board's position.

Continuing our analysis, we soon realized that even though a move might seem primo at the first ply, there might be lethal danger lurking for Dr. Plopper at the second ply. For example, let's say that Dr. Plopper decided to make a move in column 3 because the 1-ply evaluation indicated that a three-filled pattern would be created by that move. However, a move in column 3 may set up a winning move for the human. In other words, we realized that if we didn't go to the second ply, Dr. Plopper might make what he thought was a good move, but in reality was a horrible one.

We knew that ply searches are very accurate but time consuming. Let's say that Dr. Plopper had 8 possible moves he might make in a given position. Than meant eight positional evaluations for the first ply. At the 2-ply search level, there might be as many as 8 possible responses to each of the eight 1-ply moves. Table 3.1 represents the possible evaluations which might be required in each ply. To calculate the maximum for an n-ply search, we simply add the numbers for ply searches $1-n$.

We see that for the 2-ply search, Dr. Plopper would need to evaluate 72 potential positions ($8 + 8 \times 8$) to know that he was not moving into a trap. Reasoning further, we theorized that although a 2-ply search would tell if Dr. Plopper were immediately walking the plank, it would not tell him if he would be setting up a combination for the human which would lead to a win. We groaned. Determining if a move by Dr. Plopper would set up a combination required a minimum of a 4-ply search, 4680 positions, according to Table 3.1.

Computers are good at moving and evaluating data in program consciousness, but evaluating a potential of 4680 positions to determine if Dr. Plopper were moving into a trap set by the human would take time. God forbid if the human combination took 6 or more moves. If Dr. Plopper had to go 6-ply deep, the numbers would be daunting—299,592 positions!

At this moment a collective light bulb went off in our heads. We knew that using program instinct is quick, but the technique has limitations, because accurate projected human responses to Dr. Plopper's moves are unknown. We estimated that a few ply searches would probably not weaken the performance objective to have the Dr. Plopper move in a humanlike time frame. The 299,592 positional evaluations required at the 6-ply level did seem daunting.

Ah, learning.... Here's where the absolute power of learning could come into play. We reasoned that we didn't need to kill ourselves to build the most powerful program instinct into Dr. Plopper because if s/he could learn from her/his losses then the deep ply searching would not be needed. We decided that finding a balance between the contribution of program instinct and learning would prove to be the key to our implementing a powerful implementation of the OAI paradigm in the Drop Four program.

3.5 Summary

Chapter 3 began by describing four-in-a-row genre board games and proceeded through the Drop Four OAI suitability queries. Once we had determined that Drop Four was suitable for being designed using the OAI paradigm, we decided to use the persona of a fictitious Dr. Plopper for Drop Four's OAI-designed code.

We then began a discussion of the analysis proper. The first branch of the analysis eventually led to the development of the forced move algorithm, and the second branch led to the development of the marker disruption algorithm. Although the implementation of these algorithms are certainly specific to the case of Drop Four, we now believe that variations of the algorithms have potential use in a wide variety of programs.

Next we plowed directly into the first part of OAI analysis, preparing to infuse Dr. Plopper's response with a humanlike feel via program instinct. At this level of analysis, the process consisted of interviewing a four-in-a-row genre game player expert (Narendra in our case) and imprinting some of his reasoning rules into early play. We discussed the positives and negatives of using program instinct and brute-force ply searching.

Our conclusion supported the notion that although brute force ply searching provides very accurate information, it can be very time consuming. On the other hand, using program instinct to generate moves would prove very time efficient, but not as powerful as those generated by ply searching.

In the end, we decided to use a minimum of ply searching and to focus on lightweight program instinct. We knew that this balance would make Dr. Plopper vulnerable to losing at the hands of a skilled player. No matter, we reasoned, because we knew that if we were able to implement powerful learning in Dr. Plopper's brain, the lack of deep ply searching would not pose a long term hazard to her/his game play.

chapter 4

OAI design of Drop Four

This chapter presents an overview of Drop Four's OAI design. The overview consists of a discussion of game play features and the eventual look and feel of the program. In reality, Drop Four's analysis, design, and implementation cycle was repeated many times before this book was written. For clarity we've decided to present the design in a straightforward fashion, with occasional allusions to the nonlinear reality of Drop Four's project development.

4.1 Transition from analysis to design

At this point, we restated the logic of the previously generated line of analysis and added a design statement to both the first and second branches of Drop Four's analysis.

Design—branch 1

What type of data does the Drop Four program generate? The players produce records of moves. What is a move composed of? It is composed of numbers representing the column where the piece was dropped and whether the move was forced by the human to prevent a loss by Dr. Plopper. What can we do with the move list? We can determine

Dr. Plopper's last move. What can we do with Dr. Ploppers's last move? We can trace back to determine a move which would have prevented the loss. How can we find the move which guided the game to a loss for Dr. Plopper?

Design: We can assume that the last move Dr. Plopper makes will be forced to prevent allowing the human to make a move and win. In all likelihood, the last few of Dr. Plopper's moves will be forced. At some point before the final string of Dr. Plopper's moves, there must be a move that could be altered such that it would change the course of the game.

Design—branch 2

What type of data does the Drop Four program generate? The players produce records of moves. What can we do with the move list? We can reconstruct the game board position after each of the moves. What can we do with the game board positions? We can evaluate the relative strength of the players' positions. What is a position composed of? We can view the game board position as being composed of a series of piece patterns. What can we do with the comparison of the players' move lists and the game board patterns? We can calculate which game board piece patterns will lead to a loss for Dr. Plopper. How can we teach Dr. Plopper to avoid the game board patterns which repeat previous losses?

Design: We can check the patterns that are being formed on Drop Four's board as the game develops. If Dr. Plopper could recognize that a dangerous piece pattern was beginning to form, s/he could take action by making moves to disrupt the undesirable patterns.

4.2 Historical notes

Although we had design goals, implementing the design took considerable time and discussion. We decided to take a break from the analysis of program instinct and look at learning. Since we decided that the algorithms which facilitate program learning are unique to each program, we suspected that a good first step in developing learning algorithms would be to explore the fundamental nature of the data produced by Drop Four. We knew that it would be easy to keep track of the move list, the sequence of moves. In addition, we saw that each move created a new board position. Since there are 64 squares in the Drop Four game board and there are 64 possible moves, the potential maximum data record size for each game could run 64 moves + (64 × 64) potential positions, or 4160 bytes.

Two questions immediately arose. Could we develop learning algorithms from the available data? Were there any ways available to manage the data in a more efficient fashion?

Analyzing Drop Four program learning—move list data

At the beginning of the algorithm development phase Len decided to call his friend and mentor, Marc Neuberger (Ph.D.) and pose the following question, "Marc, if Narendra and I created a record of all the game's moves, we could teach the game how to learn to avoid the loss, right?"

"Len, the problem lies not in creating a record of the game's moves; the problem is finding the *kiss of death* move and if the move could be found, finding a move which would avert losing a second time with an identical sequence of moves." Marc didn't express at that time that he was certain that Narendra and Len weren't up to the task.

"Cool," Len said.

The search for the kiss of death move became our Holy Grail.

As we began to explore the move list data we knew that it would also provide piece position data. We wondered whether there were any additional data available which could aid our search to create learning. The first light bulb went off. Wham!

We realized that some moves were forced, meaning that if Dr. Plopper didn't make a certain move s/he would lose the game. Figure 4.1 shows the move list for a simple game. The third column indicates if Dr. Plopper's move was forced: 0 means that the move was not forced, 1 means that it was. The human's winning diagonal runs in the SW–NE direction.

Note the arrow that points from the human's column 3 move to Dr. Plopper's column 8 move. In this case, if Dr. Plopper had made the column 3 move instead of the column 8 move, the soon-to-follow loss would have been averted. After Dr. Plopper had lost this game, the forced move algorithm would determine that a move to column 3 was proper, and not to column 8. When a game was played having an identical (or mirrored) move sequence, Dr. Plopper would identify the sequence of moves (via the record held in the program subsonscious) and make the column 3 (or proper mirrored column 3 or column 6) move instead of the column 8 move. The loss would be averted via program learning. Figure 4.1 shows the final position of this game.

It dawned on us that if Dr. Plopper made the human's kiss of death move, the one that sets up the losing forced move sequence, the loss would be averted. In Figure 4.2, you'll note that Dr. Plopper's final move into column 3 has prevented the human's

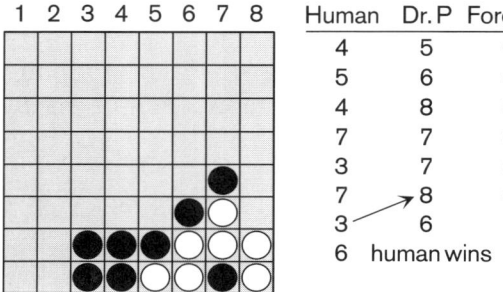

Figure 4.1 Human (Black) wins this time.

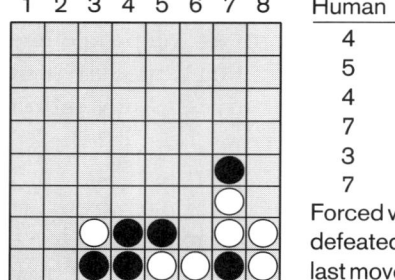

Figure 4.2 Forced move algorithm succeeds.

horizontal three-filled pattern from forming on row 2 from column 3 through column 5. Once the three-filled pattern has been defeated, Dr. Plopper is no longer forced to make a move in column 6 to prevent a loss. If the human chooses to make a move in column 6, setting up a win on the SW–NE diagonal, Dr. Plopper can avert it by simply making a column 6 move.

The forced move algorithm seemed so elegant and simple. Based on our initial analysis, it seemed like a solid method to alter the course of game play to demonstrate learning. Further analysis, however, clearly showed that although the forced move algorithm did indeed find the kiss of death move in many move sequence analyses, it was not robust enough to cover them all.

Figure 4.3 gives a move list which clearly demonstrates the limitation of the forced move algorithm in Drop Four. The game play defeats the forced move algorithm because both three-filled patterns are in the same column and above one another. If this double vertical three-filled winning pattern forms it's all over for the good doctor.

The failure of the forced move algorithm becomes clear when you examine the last three moves that the human makes. They are all in column 6. Note that the arrow

4.2 HISTORICAL NOTES

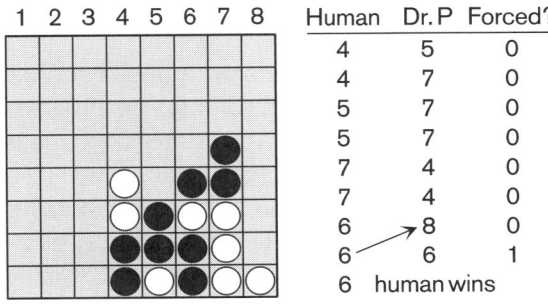

Figure 4.3 Forced move algorithm fails.

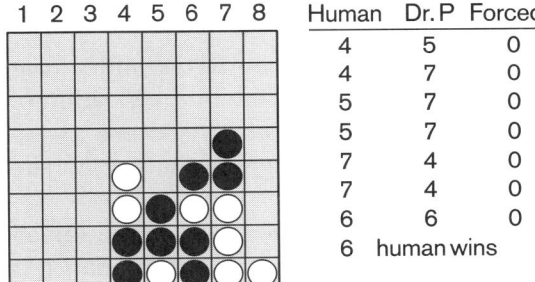

Figure 4.4 Final position of defeat of forced move algorithm.

showing the forced move switch tells Dr. Plopper to replace a column 8 move with a column 6 move. In this case, the forced move algorithm helps the human do her/his dirty work. Instead of playing three column 6 moves in a row, the human needs to play only two column 6 moves because Dr. Plopper dumbly plays a column 6 move.

Figure 4.4 shows the sorry state of affairs for Dr. Plopper after the forced move algorithm was used to generate a move from the list in Figure 4.3. It's ugly, indeed!

At this point, we deemed that although the forced move algorithm was not as robust as we would have wished, it was important enough to include in Drop Four's design cycle.

Reality intervenes

At this point, we had a working version of Drop Four up and running under DOS. This early version generated moves using program instinct. Although Dr. Plopper played tough, he could be beaten by many skilled players after a few games. We then designed and implemented the forced move algorithm and asked beta testers to first beat Dr. Plopper using their favorite move sequence and then try a second time using the same move sequence.

Brett's (the initial beta tester) response proved tremendously encouraging. The first time Dr. Plopper made a move to avert a previously experienced loss, he blurted, "What the !@#$?" and slammed his palm on the computer table. We immediately saw the power of learning.

Brett furiously began searching for other winning combinations, and as soon as he found one that Dr. Plopper could not avert a second time he called us over and gleefully exclaimed, "Hey boys! Call me when Dr. Plopper doesn't play like a ditz."

Analyzing Drop Four program learning—memory markers

We knew that saving the board position for each move would be too memory consumptive for a real-world strategy game. The answer, of course, lay in the creation of memory markers. The problem would center on the issue of which data to use to create the markers. Initially, a sensible path seemed to dictate a post game analysis, where we would try to generate a memory marker.

We reasoned that we wouldn't need memory markers for times where the forced move algorithm worked. Figure 4.4 shows a board position where the human has moved first and the forced move algorithm has failed.

We decided to draw a rectangle around the area of the game board in which the human win has been implemented. We noticed that this data set was considerably smaller than the entire 64-square board. This was our first attempt to develop a memory marker. The next step was to figure out what to do with that marker.

Our first thought was to disrupt the creation of this marker if it started to appear a second time in a game played at a later time. Of course, if there were, say, 8 squares in the marker a natural question arose. At what level of completion should the marker be disrupted? 10%? 30%? 80%? Although we strongly felt that marker disruption would be an effective strategy in learning, we didn't find any way to figure out at what level of completion a marker should be disrupted. We eventually called this learning algorithm *marker disruption*.

Reality intervenes

We decided to once again hold off on analysis and implement a first look at the memory marker disruption algorithm. The results were quite promising. There were games where the forced move learning algorithm failed but the marker disruption algorithm succeeded. Dr. Plopper's strength of play began to improve over time. The more times Dr. Plopper lost, the stronger her/his play became.

A return to marker analysis

Continuing our discussion, we noticed that although the initial marker was anchored to a specific game board location (a global coordinate system), each of the pieces in the marker had a relative spatial relationship (a local coordinate system). That understood, we realized that if we could save the memory marker data using a local coordinate system, we could abstract the marker and dramatically increase the scope of its usefulness. Once the light shone on creating the marker using relative local coordinate data, we soon realized that we could rotate the local coordinate data by 180 degrees, which would create marker mirrors. This generalizes the learning to situations never experienced.

We also saw that the forced move algorithm could benefit from the 180-degree reflection of move sequence data.

4.3 Selecting programming environment and tools

Let's begin by looking at some high level system design considerations. Once in a while, we fantasized that Drop Four would become good enough to bring to the commercial market (which has happened at the time of this writing—Trickle Down has been released for OS/2 Warp version 3). Len jumped on the OS/2 bandwagon early in the 32-bit operating system's history. Preparing the game engine so it could support different operating systems and user interface platforms seemed like a good design.

Another factor to consider was that Narendra had familiarity with DOS character mode programming. Len had familiarity with character mode DOS, Windows, and OS/2 Presentation Manager programming.

After a short discussion, we decided to write Drop Four's move generation source code in ANSI C using operating system platform-independent coding techniques. We agreed to build the move generation code using Borland's C++ compiler in a character mode DOS environment for the following reasons:

- The Borland C++ DOS compiler is fast.
- Narendra and Len both had DOS development stations at home. (Only Len had OS/2 development tools.)
- Borland's character mode DOS debugger works well.

Designing Drop Four game play features

Since we had an eye on producing a commercial quality strategy game, it seemed sensible to have several levels of difficulty for game play. They are: new beginner, beginner, intermediate, and advanced. The new beginner level is characterized by randomly generated moves. We reasoned that when Dr. Plopper plays randomly, both young children and older players getting used to the user interface can get a feel for game play, and quickly achieve a win.

On the beginner level, Dr. Plopper makes moves based on general principles, such as forming three-filled markers or thwarting the human's potential winning move if one existes. In addition, we decided to permit Dr. Plopper to find and make the winning move if the human did not block it. Note that the process of creating three-filled markers and making a winning move can be construed of as being offensive strategies, whereas blocking a potential human win is a defensive strategy.

Dr. Plopper's game play takes another step forward in the intermediate level. Using the skills of the beginner level as a baseline, we added the ability to set up 4-ply winning combinations. This feature forces the human to improve her/his game play by searching ahead to locate winning and losing combinations. The intermediate level provides a nice challenge for players of all skill levels.

We added powerful learning features to Dr. Plopper at the advanced level. Every time Dr. Plopper loses to a human s/he will learn from the experience and avoid a loss in the same fashion the next time around.

Designing move selection sequence

Since Dr. Plopper's OAI-designed move generation engine (problem domain) is platform independent, we needed to come up with a design for the DOS user interface (human interface) component which would call functions in the move generation engine. Here's a simple representation of our design:

```
BEGIN ENDLESS LOOP
    IF first play is human
        Get human move
    ENDIF
    IF game is over AND game difficulty is advanced
        Display "game over" message
        Analyze why Dr. Plopper lost
        Place results of analysis in program subconscious
        BREAK from endless loop
    ENDIF
```

```
        Get Dr. Plopper's move
    IF game is over
            Display Dr. Plopper win message
            BREAK from endless loop
    ENDIF
    IF second player is human
            Get human move
    ENDIF
RETURN to start of ENDLESS LOOP
```

Designing Drop Four program instinct

Including program instinct in a program's design will facilitate humanlike responses. In the case of a game, simulating a humanlike response can greatly increase the human opponent's pleasure in playing the game. The tough decision we needed to consider was where we should stop program instinct and begin learning. For example, if we decided to code deep ply searches into program instinct, that would slow down the time required for move generation. If we added too little program instinct, we worried that too much of a burden would be placed on learning.

Since we had declared Narendra the four-in-a-row expert, we decided to begin developing program instinct by interviewing him during his move selection process. At this level of interview we were just interested in learning the order of his decision framework for move selection. Narendra's reasoning went something like this:

1. If a winning move exists for me, make that move (offense).
2. If a winning move exists for my opponent, block that move (defense).
3. Look to set up a winning combination for me (offense).
4. Look to disrupt a winning combination for my opponent (defense).
5. Look to create three-filled markers (offense).
6. Look to disrupt three-filled markers for the opponent (defense).

We immediately noticed that there was an alternation between offensive and defensive tendencies. At which point should program learning take place? We reasoned that making a winning move and blocking a win for the opponent should be at the very top of the move selection strategies. These 1-ply searches execute very quickly and are very accurate.

Setting up winning combinations also involved limited ply searching techniques. Since ply searching provides very accurate information, we decided to include the code for managing combinations if they don't cost too much time in the move selection scheme.

Creating three-filled memory markers, on the other hand, does not involve ply searches. The algorithm simply evaluates the current position and does not examine the results of the move. Since program learning would be the result of insightful analysis of Dr. Plopper's losses, it seemed reasonable to put moves generated by program learning before program instinct to create three-filled markers.

Our program design began to shape up like this:

1. If a winning move exists for me, make that move (offense).
2. If a winning move exists for my opponent, block that move (defense).
3. Look to set up a winning combination for me (offense).
4. Look to disrupt a winning combination for my opponent (defense).
5. If game play heading for a previously experienced loss, make move selection based on program learning,
   OR
   if human game play heading for a previously experienced loss, make move selection based on program learning (offense).
6. Look to create three-filled markers (offense).
7. Look to disrupt three-filled markers for the opponent (defense).

Designing Drop Four program learning

Our view is that the first step in the design of any learning algorithm must be to look at the fundamental nature of the data produced by the program. We wanted learning that took place during game play to carry over to games that would be played after the Drop Four program had been terminated. That necessitated saving the data generated by the forced move and three-filled pattern disruption algorithms. Since file I/O is slower than transferring data from the program subconscious to the program conscious, we decided to load the program subconscious data stored on file into the computer's program subconscious at one fell swoop.

We could then relocate the data from program subconscious to program conscious at processor speed, so learning-generated moves would be made in a timely fashion. In addition, we decided to store additional learning-generated records to the program subconscious and save the data record of the program subconscious to disk when Drop Four was terminated.

The forced move algorithm is based on the record of the moves for a game. It loosely goes like this:

IF *the human has won the game*
    Save move list to data record

> *Start at the last move Dr. Plopper made, and trace back until the first unforced move is found. Replace that move with the human's move immediately preceding it.*
> *Store the index number of the altered move in the program subconscious.*

END IF

The record generated by the forced move algorithm would be stored in the program subconscious, and then could be evaluated right after each human move. If Dr. Plopper noted that the move list currently being generated was following the same path as a game which had been previously lost, s/he could look at the index indicating which move should be altered and then make that move when the game move counter reaches the appropriate value.

The three-filled pattern disruption algorithm works in a related fashion. Let's have a look:

IF *the human has won the game*
> *Save move list to data record*
> *Isolate the portion of the game board where the human's win has occurred. Dissect the area of the game board near the winning four-in-a-row pattern for any other of the human's pieces that are in a three-filled pattern.*
> *Save the area of the game board in the region of the four-in-a-row human win as a memory marker.*
> *Store the memory marker into the program subconscious.*

END IF

The three-filled marker disruption algorithm could be integrated into Dr. Plopper's move generation scheme by using what has been traditionally described as pattern recognition. As a game progresses, Dr. Plopper could compare the memory markers created by the three-filled marker disruption algorithm with pieces on the game board. Obviously, Dr. Plopper would have to disrupt the human's pattern before it was 100% complete. We decided to write a memory marker recognition function which determines if, say, 60% of the memory marker has been formed. If so, a move is generated which disrupts the pattern.

4.4 Summary

This chapter began by discussing the programming environment for Drop Four's development. Ultimately we decided to go with Borland's C/C++ compiler to create a

DOS character mode version of the game. We selected Borland's tools because the compiler is very quick and Turbo Debugger is more than adequate for our needs on this project. We also decided to use platform coding techniques to ease the task of porting the move generation section of the code to other operating systems and graphical front ends.

We used Narendra's expertise to begin the design of Drop Four's AI persona, Dr. Plopper. Interviewing an expert proved to be a good way to explore how a human who is skilled at a specified task operates. We used Narendra's knowledge and playing style in four-in-a-row genre games as the basis for our design of program instinct.

We used the data record which reflected the moves of a game of Drop Four as the basis for the forced move algorithm. This algorithm suggested that by examining the sequence of moves we would be able to find a kiss of death move and teach Dr. Plopper not to make it again.

As Narendra looked to develop three-filled patterns during game play, we reasoned that we might be able to use them to facilitate learning. The process would be to examine a board after game play had terminated, locate three-filled patterns, and convert them into memory markers. Once the memory markers were transferred to the program subconscious they could be used by Dr. Plopper at a later time. We reasoned that since the three-filled patterns played a role in the human's defeating Dr. Plopper, we would probably be able to use the memory markers to disrupt the three-filled patterns before they were formed. We called this algorithm three-filled marker disruption.

chapter 5

Drop Four's DOS platform move selection

This chapter contains code snippets from the file game.c, which is located on the disk provided with the book. Although this file does not contain any OAI-generated code, it will provide a look at how the OAI code integrates into code running in a nonpreemptive single-threaded real-mode operating system.

Note that the comments to the source code snippets in the text will prove richer than the comments in the source files provided on the disk. We have intentionally bolstered the comments to improve the readability of the most important portions of the code.

5.1 Define statements and function map

We begin by presenting the source code to the header file called game.h. This file contains a list of #define statements which will facilitate your understanding of the code presentation. We strongly suggest that you glance at the #define statements in Listing 5.1. Here's why: a few years back Len received a phone call from a reader who expressed anger at not knowing what a UCHAR was. Len patiently explained that the unsigned chararacter was defined as UCHAR in a header file which was presented in the text. The reader remained furious and strongly suggested that Len should highlight the #define statements early in the code presentation. Listing 5.1 does just that.

❑ **Listing 5.1**   #define statements.

```
#ifndef TRUE
#define TRUE              1
#endif

#ifndef FALSE
#define FALSE             0
#endif

#ifndef UCHAR
#define UCHAR unsigned char
#endif

#ifndef SHORT
#define SHORT short int
#endif

#define PLAYER_VS_COMPUTER    0
#define COMPUTER_VS_PLAYER    1
#define PLAYER_VS_PLAYER      2
#define COMPUTER_VS_COMPUTER  3
#define HUMAN                 0
#define COMPUTER              1
#define FIRST                 0
#define SECOND                1

#define STANDARD_PLAY         0
#define FLIP_BOARD_OVER       1
#define CIRCLE_BOARD_LEFT     2
#define ELECT_BOARD_MOVE      3
#define RANDOM_BOARD_MOVE     4

#define RED_BUTTON            RED
#define BLUE_BUTTON           BLUE
#define RED_AND_BLUE          9
#define WIN                   1
#define LOSS                  0
#define DRAW                  9
```

5.1 DEFINE STATEMENTS AND FUNCTION MAP

```
#define BAD_MOVE              251
#define GOOD_MOVE             250

#define LEFT_90               1
#define RIGHT_90              2
#define TURN_180              3

#define NEW_BEGINNER          0
#define BEGINNER              1
#define INTERMEDIATE          2
#define ADVANCED              3
#define EXPERT                4

#define NO_ROTATION           0
#define ROTATE_LEFT_90        1
#define ROTATE_RIGHT_90       2
#define FLIP_180              3

#define INFO_OPTION           0
#define START_OPTION          1
#define OPTIONS_OPTION        2
#define PLAYERS_OPTION        3
#define DIFFICULTY_OPTION     4
#define HELP_OPTION           5
#define QUIT_OPTION           6

#define BLACK                 0
#define BLUE                  1
#define GREEN                 2
#define CYAN                  3
#define RED                   4
#define MAGENTA               5
#define BROWN                 6
#define WHITE                 7
#define NORMAL                7
#define REVERSE               112
#define ON_INTENSITY          8
#define OFF_INTENSITY         0
#define ON_BLINK              128
#define OFF_BLINK             0

#define NO_IMMEDIATE_LOSS     200
#define NO_IMMEDIATE_WIN      201
#define NO_FORK_FOUND         202
```

```
#define FORK_FOUND              203
#define NO_BOOK_MOVE            204
#define NO_PATTERN_DETECTED     205
#define PLACE_IN_COFFIN         206
#define NO_FORCE_WIN            207
#define NO_SETUP_FOUND          208
#define BE_PASSIVE              209
#define NO_ADVANTAGE            210
#define NO_DOUBLE_PATTERN       211
#define NO_FIRST_PLY_MOVE       212
#define NO_MATCHING_RECORD      213
#define NO_WINNING_PATTERN      214
#define NO_HUMAN_WIN            215
#define NO_END_GAME_MOVE        216
#define NO_MORE_SEQUENCE        217 ■
```

Listings 5.2 through 5.10 provide a list of functions by C source file. The complete source code for these files will be found on the book's diskette. This map of functions has been provided to facilitate your quickly locating the source files if need be.

❑ **Listing 5.2**   game.c function list.

```
void       main( void )
void       draw_buttons( int color )
void       erase_a_button( UCHAR column )
void       start_game( UCHAR game_difficulty,
                       UCHAR first_player,
                       UCHAR second_player )
UCHAR get_human_move( void )
void       drop_piece( UCHAR column,
                       UCHAR turn )
void       draw_piece( int row,
                       UCHAR column,
                       UCHAR turn, UCHAR flag )
void       initialize_game( void )
void       draw_board( void )
UCHAR generate_random_move( void )
UCHAR generate_first_move( void )
int        is_there_a_winner( UCHAR first_player,
                              UCHAR second_player )
void       display_game_settings( RECT *R,
                                  UCHAR game_difficulty,
                                  UCHAR game_options )
```

5.1 DEFINE STATEMENTS AND FUNCTION MAP

```
void       print_byte( char pr )
void       print_string( char *str )
void       print_moves( void )
void       report_move( char *str )  ■
```

❏ **Listing 5.3**   engine.c function list.

```
UCHAR get_computer_move( UCHAR game_difficulty,
                         UCHAR turn )
UCHAR do_random_move( void )
UCHAR check_for_loss( UCHAR turn )
UCHAR check_for_win( UCHAR turn )
void       init_coffin( void )
void       create_coffin( UCHAR turn )
void       create_coffin_o( UCHAR opponent )
UCHAR ghost1_coffin( UCHAR turn )
UCHAR ghost3_coffin( UCHAR turn )
UCHAR look_ahead( UCHAR turn )
UCHAR look_ahead_opp( UCHAR turn )
UCHAR search_ghost1_fork_move( UCHAR turn )
UCHAR search_ghost2_fork_move( UCHAR turn )
UCHAR look_force_win_in_2( UCHAR turn )
UCHAR search_ghost3_fork_move( UCHAR turn )
UCHAR is_ghost4_fork( UCHAR turn )
UCHAR is_ghost3_fork( UCHAR turn )
UCHAR is_coffined_out( void )
UCHAR adv_is_coffined_out( void )
void       is_setup_in_3_ply( UCHAR turn )
UCHAR stop_setup2( UCHAR turn )
UCHAR create_setup2( UCHAR turn )
UCHAR create_setup_2pat( UCHAR turn )
UCHAR stop_setup_2pat( UCHAR turn )  ■
```

❏ **Listing 5.4**   engine2.c function list.

```
void       initialize_move_list( void )
void       record_move( UCHAR move )
UCHAR number_of_squares_in_column( UCHAR column )
UCHAR number_of_squares_in_ghost1_column( UCHAR column )
UCHAR number_of_squares_in_ghost2_column( UCHAR column )
UCHAR number_of_squares_in_ghost3_column( UCHAR column )
UCHAR number_of_squares_in_ghost4_column( UCHAR column )
UCHAR number_of_squares_in_ghost5_column( UCHAR column )
```

```
void       initialize_board( void )
void       initialize_ghosts( void )
void       initialize_ghost2( void )
int        search_board( void )
int        search3_ghost2( void )
int        search_ghost1( void )
int        search_ghost2( void )
int        search_ghost3( void )
int        search_ghost4( void )
int        search_ghost5( void )
void       copy_board_to_ghost1( void )
void       copy_ghost1_to_ghost2( void )
void       copy_ghost2_to_ghost3( void )
void       copy_ghost3_to_ghost4( void )
void       copy_ghost4_to_ghost5( void )
void       copy_ghost5_to_ghost6( void )
void       copy_ghost6_to_ghost5( void )
UCHAR is_ghost2_fork( UCHAR turn ) ■
```

❏ **Listing 5.5**   engine3.c function list.

```
UCHAR do_positional_move( UCHAR turn )
UCHAR opening_book_first( UCHAR turn )
UCHAR opening_book_defense( UCHAR turn )
UCHAR opening_book_offense( UCHAR turn )
UCHAR pattern_search_board( UCHAR turn )
UCHAR pattern_search_ghost1( UCHAR turn )
UCHAR check_for_pattern( UCHAR turn ) ■
```

❏ **Listing 5.6**   engine4.c function list.

```
void       create_win_board( void )
void       create_win_ghost1( void )
void       create_win_ghost2( void )
void       create_win_ghost3( void )
UCHAR forced_win_board( UCHAR turn )
UCHAR double_win_in_column( UCHAR turn )
void       coffin_corner( UCHAR turn )
void       coffin_pattern( UCHAR turn )
UCHAR create_double_pattern( UCHAR turn )
UCHAR count_double_board( UCHAR turn )
UCHAR count_double_ghost1( UCHAR turn )
UCHAR count_double_ghost2( UCHAR turn )
UCHAR count_double_ghost3( UCHAR turn ) ■
```

5.1 DEFINE STATEMENTS AND FUNCTION MAP

❏ **Listing 5.7**   engine5.c function list.

```
void      check_aggression( UCHAR turn )
UCHAR aggression4( UCHAR turn )
UCHAR aggression3( UCHAR turn )
UCHAR aggression1( UCHAR turn )
UCHAR aggression4a( UCHAR turn )
UCHAR aggression3a( UCHAR turn )
UCHAR aggression2a( UCHAR turn )
UCHAR aggression1a( UCHAR turn )
UCHAR aggression5a( UCHAR turn )
UCHAR aggression6a( UCHAR turn )  ■
```

❏ **Listing 5.8**   engine6.c function list.

```
void      evaluate_board( UCHAR turn,
                          UCHAR order )
UCHAR first_ply_move(UCHAR turn,
                          UCHAR flags[8] )  ■
```

❏ **Listing 5.9**   engine7.c function list.

```
void      close_data_base( void )
void      open_data_base( void )
void      add_move_list( void )
void      first_move_analysis( void )
void      second_move_analysis( void )
void      second_move_comp_analysis( void )
UCHAR first_move_check( UCHAR moves_offset )
UCHAR second_move_check( UCHAR moves_offset )
void      off_first_move_analysis( void )
void      off_second_move_analysis( void )
void      off_second_move_comp_analysis( void )
UCHAR off_first_move_check( UCHAR moves_offset )
UCHAR off_second_move_check( UCHAR moves_offset )
UCHAR first_human_win( UCHAR moves_offset )
UCHAR second_human_win( UCHAR moves_offset )
UCHAR off_first_human_win( UCHAR moves_offset )
UCHAR off_second_human_win( UCHAR moves_offset )
void      opponent_type_move( UCHAR opponent )
void      opponent_type_move_comp( UCHAR opponent )
void      add_patttern_list( void )
void      first_pat_analysis( UCHAR turn )
```

```
UCHAR find_winning_pattern( UCHAR turn, int pattern_start )
UCHAR first_openings( UCHAR sequence, UCHAR moves_offset )
void       add_sequence( void )
void       write_end_board( void )
UCHAR off_end_move_check( UCHAR moves_offset )
UCHAR end_move_check( UCHAR moves_offset )
UCHAR off_human_move_check( UCHAR moves_offset )
UCHAR human_move_check( UCHAR moves_offset ) ∎
```

❏ **Listing 5.10**   engine8.c function list.

```
UCHAR calculate_end( UCHAR turn, UCHAR double_pat_key )
UCHAR calculate_end_ghost1( UCHAR turn, UCHAR double_pat_key )
UCHAR check_end_game_over( UCHAR turn )
void       create_2pat_flags( UCHAR turn )
void       create_2pat_flags_ghost1( UCHAR turn )
UCHAR check_end_game( UCHAR turn )
void       add_end_game_comp( UCHAR turn, UCHAR move )
void       add_end_game_human( UCHAR opponent ) ∎
```

5.2 *In the beginning*

All C programs begin with the function main(). Since we do not use any command line parameters and are not returning any variables to the calling program, we use void as a parameter and for the function return type. Listing 5.11 presents a look at the portion of the main() function which manages Drop Four game play options, including starting the game. Note that we have tried to use very descriptive function names. We've added comments to those function calls whose names we don't feel tell the whole story.

❏ **Listing 5.11**   Source code managing the setting of Drop Four game play options.

```
// Menu loop.

e_flag = 0;

do
    {
```

5.2 IN THE BEGINNING

```c
      // Display menubar.

      if( menubarEvent( MB1, &event ) ) {

         switch(event) {

            case 0:

               // Open first drop down window.

               ret_val= openDropDown( MB1,
                                      0,
                                      DD0,
                                      DD0_key );

               switch( ret_val ) {

                     // Display game information menu.

                     case INFO_OPTION:

                        openMessage( game_mess,
                                     WHITE,
                                     BLUE,
                                     WHITE,
                                     GREEN );
                        break;
                     }
                  }
            break;

            case START_OPTION:

               // Wait 100 ms.

               delay( 100 );

               // Game initialization.

               initialize_game();
```

```
        // Display the game settings.

        display_game_settings( ( struct RECT * )R2,
                               game_difficulty,
                               first_player,
                               second_player );

        // This function provides the entry point to
        // playing the game and all the OAI-developed
        // functions.

        start_game( game_difficulty,
                    first_player,
                    second_player);
        break;

    case OPTIONS_OPTION:

        // Open second drop down window.

        ret_val= openDropDown( MB1,
                               event,
                               DD2,
                               DD2_key );

        // Process selected item.

        switch(ret_val) {

            // Print the list of moves.

            case 0:

                print_string(heading);
                print_string(crlf);
                print_string(bar);
                print_string(crlf);
                print_string(crlf);
                print_moves();
                break;

                // Set debugging flag so debugging info
                // (Dr. Plopper's comp-mental activity)
                // will be displayed on the game screen.
```

5.2 IN THE BEGINNING

```
            case 1:
               debugging= 1;
               break;

            case 2:
               debugging= 0;

               // Draw debugging screen pattern.

               for( row= 1; row < 25; row++ ) {
                  for( column= 0; column < 80; column++ ) {
                     vdChar( row,
                             column,
                             mkToken( 176,
                                      screen_attr ) );
                  }
               }
               break;
            }
         break;

     case PLAYERS_OPTION:

         // Open third drop down window.

         ret_val= openDropDown( MB1,
                                event,
                                DD1,
                                DD1,
                                DD1_key);

         // Process item selection.

         switch( ret_val ) {

            case PLAYER_VS_COMPUTER:
               first_player= HUMAN;
               second_player= COMPUTER;
               break;

            case COMPUTER_VS_PLAYER:
               first_player= COMPUTER;
               second_player= HUMAN;
               break;
```

```
         case PLAYER_VS_PLAYER:
            first_player= HUMAN;
            second_player= HUMAN;
            break;

         case COMPUTER_VS_COMPUTER:
            first_player= COMPUTER;
            second_player= COMPUTER;
            break;

         }
         break;

   case DIFFICULTY_OPTION:

      // Open fourth drop down window.

      ret_val= openDropDown( MB1,
                             event,
                             DD4,
                             DD4_key);

      // Process item selection.

      switch(ret_val) {

         case NEW_BEGINNER:
            game_difficulty= NEW_BEGINNER;
            break;

         case BEGINNER:
            game_difficulty= BEGINNER;
            break;

         case INTERMEDIATE:
            game_difficulty= INTERMEDIATE;
            break;

         case ADVANCED:
            game_difficulty= ADVANCED;
            break;
         }
      break;
```

5.2 IN THE BEGINNING

```
            // No help installed in the DOS version at this time.

            case HELP_OPTION:
               break;

            case QUIT_OPTION:

               // Write the forced move memory and
               // three-filled marker disruption data
               // to the hard disk.

               close_data_base();
               e_flag= 1;
               break;
         }
      }
   } while(!e_flag); ∎
```

The function

```
    void draw_buttons( int color );
```

draws the buttons at the top of the game board. The user moves the text mouse cursor over a button and makes a move by clicking once on the left mouse button.

The function

```
    void erase_a_button( UCHAR column );
```

erases the button above the game board corresponding to the value contained in `column`. This function is used to remove a button as a game piece drops into its proper place on the game board and to permanently erase a button over a column which contains 8 pieces. The button is erased when a column is filled with 8 pieces, to signify that trying to move in a filled column is in fact an illegal move.

This function initiates the start of a new game:

```
    void start_game( UCHAR game_difficulty,
                     UCHAR first_player,
                     UCHAR second_player );
```

The first parameter is `game_difficulty`. There are four levels of game play: new beginner, beginner, intermediate, and advanced. On the new beginner level, Dr. Plopper makes random moves. This is the easiest level of play. On the beginner level, Dr. Plopper uses a small amount of program instinct to build three-filled patterns and to stop human opponents from winning (1-ply search). Listing 5.12 presents the source for the start_game(...) function.

❏ **Listing 5.12**   Source code to the start_game(...) function.

```
void start_game( UCHAR game_difficulty,
                 UCHAR first_player,
                 UCHAR second_player )
{

UCHAR turn= RED_BUTTON;
UCHAR move;
int   key;
UCHAR squares[8];
int   iterations;
UCHAR end;

    do {

        // Initialize col number array.

        for( iterations= 0; iterations < 8; iterations++ ) {
           move= number_of_squares_in_column( (UCHAR) iterations );
           squares[iterations]= move;
           }

        /////////////////////////////////////////////////////////
        // The debugging info is printed to the screen
        // using the following code. This proved
        // invaluable in helping us to find flaws in
        // Dr. Plopper's thought processes.

        if(debugging) {

           mvCur(22,0);
           for(move= 0; move < 8; move++) {
              printf("%d ",coffin[move]);
              }

           mvCur(24,0);
           for(move= 0; move < 8; move++) {
              printf("%d ",squares[move]);
              }
```

5.2 IN THE BEGINNING

```
            key= 8;
            for(iterations= 0; iterations < 8; iterations++) {
               mvCur(key++,56);
               for(move= 0; move < 8; move++) {
                  printf("%X ",raw_score[iterations][move]);
               }
            }

         mvCur(18,56);
         for(move= 0; move < 8; move++) {
            printf("%02d ",def_weights[move]);
         }

         mvCur(20,56);
         for(move= 0; move < 8; move++) {
            printf("%02d ",evaluation_first_ply[move]);
         }

         if(first_player == COMPUTER) {
           end= calculate_end(turn, 4);
           }
         else {
           end= calculate_end(turn, 3);
           }

         if(end == BLUE) {
           vdWrite(6, 60, 8,"blue_end",7);
           }
         else if(end == RED) {
           vdWrite(6, 60, 8, "red_end ", 7);
           }
         else {
           vdWrite(6, 60, 8, "draw    ", 7);
           }


         key= 12;
         for( iterations= 0; iterations < 8; iterations++ ) {
            mvCur( key++ , 0 );
            for( move= 0; move < 8; move++ ) {
                printf( "%d ", win_board[iterations][move] );
               }
            }
```

```
            if( ( move_type[moves_offset-1] == 5 ) ||
                ( move_type[moves_offset-1] == 4 ) ||
                ( move_type[moves_offset-1] == 3 ) ) {
               mvCur( 22, 56 );
               printf( "record= %3d", record );
               mvCur( 23, 56 );
               printf( "subrecord= %1d",  subrecord );
               }
            else {
               mvCur( 22, 56 );
               printf( "record=     " );
               mvCur( 23,56 );
               printf("subrecord=    ");
               }

         }

      //
      // Debugging report code ends here.
      //////////////////////////////////////////////////////////

      // First player's move.

if(first_player==HUMAN) {

   // Get human move.

   do {
      move= get_human_move();

      // If the human tries to make a move in a column
      // which contains 8 game pieces, then the move
      // will be illegal. A beep indicates that another
      // move must be selected.

      if(squares[move] == 8) {
         putchar(7);
         }
      } while( squares[move] == 8 );
```

5.2 IN THE BEGINNING

```
      // Once a legal move has been selected, then
      // the button which has just been selected
      // is erased. This is to create an illusion that
      // the button which has been selected falls
      // down the column.

      erase_a_button(move);

      // Once the button is erase, the game piece
      // drops down the column until it can fall
      // no farther.

      drop_piece(move, turn);

      // Now that the move has been made, the
      // program must determine if the game has
      // ended.

      if( is_there_a_winner( first_player,
                             second_player) ) {

         // Record game statistics used in next iteration of
         // commercial game.

         record_stats( game_difficulty, WIN );
         if( ( game_difficulty == ADVANCED ) &&
             ( second_player == COMPUTER ) ) {

            // Since learning takes place only at the
            // advanced level, the learning analysis
            // developed using the OAI paradigm
            // takes place here.

            // Save game loss sequences.

            // Forced move algorithm.
            // Change the first unforced move before the loss.

            first_move_analysis();
```

```
            // Save the level of the analysis, the move to be
            // changed, and the new move to defeat the loss.
            // Save the sequence of moves into program consciousness.
            // Create and save "mirrored" analysis into program
            // consciousness.

            add_move_list();

            if( second_seq_flag ) {

                // Forced move algorithm
                // changes the last move before a double threat.

                second_move_analysis();

                // Save sequence of moves into program consciousness.
                // Create and save "mirrored" analysis into program
                // consciousness.

                add_move_list();

                // Transfer record to program subconscious if the
                // program subconscious has not yet been filled.

                add_sequence();
            }

            // Create three-filled memory markers
            // and save.

            first_pat_analysis( turn );

            // Relocate the three-filled markers
            // and "mirror" program subconscious.

            add_pattern_list();
        }
    return;
    }
```

5.2 IN THE BEGINNING

```
            if(turn == RED_BUTTON) {
               turn= BLUE_BUTTON;
               draw_buttons(BLUE_BUTTON);
               }
            else {
               turn= RED_BUTTON;
               draw_buttons(RED_BUTTON);
               }
         }
      else {

         // Get computer move and pass difficulty level.

         vdWrite( 4,
                  60,
                  0,
                  "Thinking...",
                  mkAttr( BLUE,
                          WHITE,
                          OFF_INTENSITY,
                          ON_BLINK ) );

         move= get_computer_move_first(game_difficulty, turn);

         vdWrite( 4,
                  60,
                  0,
                  "           ",
                  mkAttr( BLUE,
                          WHITE,
                          OFF_INTENSITY,
                          OFF_BLINK ) );

         erase_a_button( move );

         drop_piece( move, turn );

         if( is_there_a_winner( first_player,
                                second_player ) ) {
```

```
         if( second_player == HUMAN ) {
            record_stats( game_difficulty, LOSS );
            }

         if( game_difficulty == ADVANCED ) {

            // Save game loss patterns.

            first_pat_analysis(turn);
            add_pattern_list();
            }

      if( ( game_difficulty == ADVANCED ) &&
          ( second_player == COMPUTER ) ) {
          first_move_analysis();

          add_move_list();

          add_sequence();

          if( second_seq_flag ) {

             second_move_comp_analysis();

             add_move_list();

             add_sequence();
             }
          }
      return;
      }

   if( turn == RED_BUTTON ) {
      turn= BLUE_BUTTON;
      draw_buttons( BLUE_BUTTON );
      }
   else {
      turn= RED_BUTTON;
      draw_buttons( RED_BUTTON );
      }
   }

delay( 100 );
```

5.2 IN THE BEGINNING

```
   for( iterations= 0; iterations < 8; iterations++ ) {
      move= number_of_squares_in_column( ( UCHAR ) iterations );
      squares[iterations]= move;
      }

////////////////////////////////////////////
// Debugging info.
if( debugging ) {

   mvCur( 22, 0 );
   for( move= 0; move < 8; move++ ) {
      printf( "%d ", coffin[move] );
      }

   mvCur( 24, 0 );
   for( move= 0; move < 8; move++ ) {
      printf( "%d ", squares[move] );
      }

   key= 3;
   for( iterations= 0; iterations < 8; iterations++ ) {
      mvCur( key++,0 );
      for( move= 0; move < 8; move++ ) {
         printf( "%d ",board[iterations][move] );
         }
      }

   key= 8;
   for( iterations= 0; iterations < 8; iterations++ ) {
      mvCur( key++,56 );
      for( move= 0; move < 8; move++ ) {
         printf( "%X ",raw_score[iterations][move] );
         }
      }

   mvCur( 18,56 );
   for( move= 0; move < 8; move++ ) {
      printf( "%02d ",off_weights[move] );
      }

   mvCur( 20,56 );
   for( move= 0; move < 8; move++ ) {
      printf( "%02d ",evaluation_first_ply[move] );
      }
```

```
      if( turn == COMPUTER ) {
        end= calculate_end( turn, 4 );
        }
      else {
        end= calculate_end( turn, 3 );
        }

      if( end == BLUE ) {
        vdWrite( 6, 60, 8,"blue_end",7 );
        }
      else if( end == RED ) {
        vdWrite( 6, 60, 8, "red_end ", 7 );
        }
      else {
        vdWrite( 6, 60, 8, "draw    ", 7 );
        }

      key= 12;
      for( iterations= 0; iterations < 8; iterations++ ) {
        mvCur( key++,0 );
        for( move= 0; move < 8; move++ ) {
          printf( "%d ",win_board[iterations][move] );
          }
        }

      if( ( move_type[moves_offset-1] == 5  ) ||
          ( move_type[moves_offset-1] == 4  ) ||
          ( move_type[moves_offset-1] == 3  ) ) {
        mvCur( 22,56 );
        printf( "record= %3d", record );
        mvCur( 23,56 );
        printf( "subrecord= %1d", subrecord );
        }
      else {
        mvCur( 22,56 );
        printf( "record=    " );
        mvCur( 23,56 );
        printf( "subrecord=    " );
        }
    }
//
///////////////////////////////////////
```

5.2 IN THE BEGINNING

```c
      // Second player's move.
      if( second_player==HUMAN ) {

         // Get human move.

         do {
            move= get_human_move( );
            if( squares[move] == 8 ) {
               putchar( 7 );
               }
            } while( squares[move] == 8 );

         if( move == 'Q' ) {

            break;
            }

         erase_a_button( move );

         drop_piece( move, turn );

         if( is_there_a_winner( first_player, second_player ) ) {

            record_stats( game_difficulty, WIN );

            if( ( game_difficulty==ADVANCED ) &&
                ( first_player==COMPUTER ) ) {

            // Save game loss sequences.

              off_first_move_analysis( );

              add_move_list( );

              if( second_seq_flag ) {

                 off_second_move_analysis( );

                 add_move_list( );

                 }
```

```
        // Save game loss patterns.

          first_pat_analysis( turn );

          add_pattern_list( );

        }
        return;
     }

     if( turn == RED_BUTTON ) {
        turn= BLUE_BUTTON;
        draw_buttons( BLUE_BUTTON );
        }
     else {
        turn= RED_BUTTON;
        draw_buttons( RED_BUTTON );
        }
  }
  else {

     // Get computer move and pass difficulty level.

     vdWrite( 4,
              60,
              0,
              "Thinking...",
              mkAttr( BLUE,
                      WHITE,
                      OFF_INTENSITY,
                      ON_BLINK ) );

     move= get_computer_move_second( game_difficulty, turn );

     vdWrite( 4,
              60,
              0,
              "           ",
              mkAttr( BLUE,
                      WHITE,
                      OFF_INTENSITY,
                      OFF_BLINK ) );
```

5.2 IN THE BEGINNING

```
      erase_a_button( move );

      drop_piece( move, turn );

      if( is_there_a_winner( first_player, second_player ) ) {

         if( first_player == HUMAN ) {

           record_stats( game_difficulty, LOSS );

          }

         if( game_difficulty==ADVANCED ) {

         // Save game win patterns.

           first_pat_analysis( turn );

           add_pattern_list(  );

          }

         if( ( game_difficulty==ADVANCED ) &&
             ( first_player==COMPUTER ) ) {

           off_first_move_analysis( );

           add_move_list( );

           if( second_seq_flag ) {

              off_second_move_comp_analysis( );

              add_move_list( );

            }
          }
        return;
       }
```

```
              if( turn == RED_BUTTON ) {
                 turn= BLUE_BUTTON;
                 draw_buttons( BLUE_BUTTON );
                 }
              else {
                 turn= RED_BUTTON;
                 draw_buttons( RED_BUTTON );
                 }
              }

        } while( move != 'Q' );

  } ■
```

The function

```
    UCHAR get_human_move( void );
```

allows the human to make a move via the mouse.

The function

```
    void drop_piece( UCHAR column,
                     UCHAR turn );
```

drops a game piece into the appropriate column. The action follows this sequence:

1. Human moves text mouse cursor over button above board.
2. Human clicks once on the left mouse button.
3. Button over game board column is erased.
4. Game piece drops down column and stops at proper spot.
5. If legal moves remain in column, button reappears.

The function

```
    void draw_piece( int   row,
                     UCHAR column,
                     UCHAR turn,
                     UCHAR flag );
```

draws a piece in a specified row and column of the game board.

The function

```
    void initialize_game( void );
```

sets the board data to zeroes.

The function

```
void draw_board( void );
```

draws the game board using the data contained in the game board array as a guide.
The function

```
UCHAR generate_random_move( void );
```

generates a random legal move between 1 and 8.
The function

```
UCHAR generate_first_move( void );
```

generates a random move between columns 3 and 6.
The method

```
int   is_there_a_winner( UCHAR first_player,
                         UCHAR second_player );
```

determines if the game has been won.
The method

```
void  display_game_settings( RECT *R,
                             UCHAR game_difficulty,
                             UCHAR game_options );
```

displays the options that have been selected by the human player. These include the game difficulty and the players.
The functions

```
void print_byte( char pr );

void print_string( char *str );

void print_moves( void );
```

are platform dependent. They use the PC's BIOS to print the move list to the printer.

5.3 Summary

This chapter presents code snippets from the game.c source file. This OS platform-dependent file makes calls to Drop Four's human interface component (HIC) and problem domain component (PDC), Dr. Plopper's compu-mind.

The source code demonstrates that when a human beats Dr. Plopper at the advanced level, two types of learning analysis take place. The forced move algorithm is used to avert certain types of sequential losses and the creation of double patterns (more on that when the code to implement forced move learning is presented). The three-filled marker disruption learning functions also are applied when the human has won. In both cases, "mirrors" to the analyzed information are created and stored in Dr. Plopper's program subconscious for use during some future game.

chapter 6

Drop Four program instinct: Basic concepts mediating move generation

This chapter presents the reasoning behind the `coffin[]` array. This array is filled with information derived early on in the move generation process which alerts Dr. Plopper to moves that might have a deleterious impact on the game. There will be times when Dr. Plopper will be alerted to the reality that making a certain move will lead to a loss, and other times when s/he will be alerted to the reality that a certain move will take away a potential weak move for the human. The fundamental idea is that Dr. Plopper should not make weak moves for either of the game's players.

    The `coffin[]` array is an integral part of Dr. Plopper's move generation functions. Chapter 7 presents the source code listing to the `get_computer_move(...)` function. Using the data contained in the `coffin[]` array speeds move selection by improving the program's efficiency.

    By determining pivotal consequences of potential moves at the beginning of Dr. Plopper's move generation scheme s/he is able to use these evaluations when selecting a move. Dr. Plopper's moves may be generated by many different functions, and each of these functions would benefit from knowing the evaluations placed in the `coffin[]` array.

6.1 The coffin[] array

The coffin[] array receives data which warns Dr. Plopper not to make certain moves. Dr. Plopper's moves are generated using two strategies, ply searches and positional evaluations. We knew that the ply search would never make a poor move in less than the depth of the ply considered in the search. The non-ply positional-evaluation generated moves might make a very dumb move, because they do not consider the human's response. That fact leaves all the non-ply positional moves vulnerable to setting up a win for the human.

The solution we chose to reduce the chance of a positionally generated move being disastrous was to evaluate all bad moves via ply search techniques before any positional move generator functions were invoked.

The coffin[] array consists of 8 elements of unsigned characters. Each element can be thought of as corresponding to one of Drop Four's game board's columns. Drop Four's columns are numbered from 1 to 8. The coffin[] array elements' values range from 0 to 7. Listing 6.1 presents the source code for the coffin[] array declaration.

❏ **Listing 6.1** Source code for the coffin[] array.

```
UCHAR coffin[8]=    { 0, 0, 0, 0, 0, 0, 0, 0 };
```
∎

The following table presents the relationship between the Drop Four game board columns and the coffin[] array element locations.

Drop Four Column	coffin[] Element
1	0
2	1
3	2
4	3
5	4
6	5
7	6
8	7

The following table presents the meaning of the data which could potentially be placed in the coffin[] array. Note that if a 4 is placed in a coffin[] array element it will lead to an almost certain win for Dr. Plopper if another piece is put in that column.

6.1 THE coffin[] ARRAY

Number	Meaning
1	Human has an immediate win or fork
2	Dr. Plopper has an immediate win or fork
3	Human has a double pattern (very advantageous)
4	Dr. Plopper has a double pattern

Listing 6.2 presents the source code for the `is_coffined_out` function. This last resort move function is reached when it has been determined that all other possible moves have potential consequences.

❑ **Listing 6.2** Source code for the `is_coffined_out(...)` function.

```
UCHAR is_coffined_out()
{
UCHAR number;
UCHAR squares[8];
UCHAR win1[8][8];
UCHAR move_list[8];
UCHAR priority[8];
int   ctr;
int   iterations;
UCHAR move, opponent;

   // Initialize column number array.

   for( iterations= 0; iterations < 8; iterations++ ) {
      squares[iterations]=
                number_of_squares_in_column( ( UCHAR ) iterations );
      }

   // If every coffin element either
   // holds number greater than 0 OR
   // the number of pieces in a column is equal to 8 ( or filled ).

   if( ((coffin[0]) || (squares[0] == 8)) &&
       ((coffin[1]) || (squares[1] == 8)) &&
       ((coffin[2]) || (squares[2] == 8)) &&
       ((coffin[3]) || (squares[3] == 8)) &&
       ((coffin[4]) || (squares[4] == 8)) &&
       ((coffin[5]) || (squares[5] == 8)) &&
       ((coffin[6]) || (squares[6] == 8)) &&
       ((coffin[7]) || (squares[7] == 8)) ) {
```

```
      // If the number of pieces in a column is less than 8 AND
      // an array element holds the value 4,
      // then return the element number.

      for(ctr= 0; ctr < 8; ctr++) {
         if((squares[ctr] < 8) && (coffin[ctr] == 4)) {
           return ctr;
            }
         }

      // If the number of pieces in a column is less than 8 AND
      // an array element holds the value 2,
      // then return the element number.

      for(ctr= 0; ctr < 8; ctr++) {
         if((squares[ctr] < 8) && (coffin[ctr] == 2)) {
           return ctr;
            }
         }

      // If the number of pieces in a column is less than 8 AND
      // an array element holds the value 3,
      // then return the element number.

      for(ctr= 0; ctr < 8; ctr++) {
         if((squares[ctr] < 8) && (coffin[ctr] == 3)) {
           return ctr;
            }
         }

      // Return the first legal move starting at element 0.

      for(ctr= 0; ctr < 8; ctr++) {
         if(squares[ctr] < 8) {
           return ctr;
            }
         }

   // There are no legal moves and the game has been drawn.

   return 8;
}  ■
```

6.2 The `init_coffin()` function

This simple function initializes the elements of the `coffin[]` array to zeroes. Listing 6.3 presents the source code for the `init_coffin(...)` function.

❏ **Listing 6.3** Source code for the `init_coffin(...)` function.

```
/////////////////////////////////////
//
// Initialize coffin buffer.
//

void init_coffin()
{
UCHAR iterations;

   // Reinitialize coffin by placing the value 0
   // in each coffin[] element.

   for(iterations= 0; iterations < 8; iterations++) {
      coffin[iterations]= 0;
      }

} ■
```

6.3 The `create_coffin(turn)` function

The `create_coffin(...)` function places a 1 in the `coffin[]` array if it determines that a move in a column will result in a guaranteed forced loss for Dr. Plopper. It provides accurate information via ply searches. Listing 6.4 presents the source code for `create_coffin(...)`.

❏ **Listing 6.4** Source code for the `create_coffin(...)` function.

```
/////////////////////////////////////
//
// Place bad moves into coffin.
//
```

```
void create_coffin(UCHAR turn)
{
UCHAR number;
UCHAR priority[8];
int   iterations, iterations1, iterations2;
UCHAR move;
UCHAR opponent;
UCHAR row, result;

   if(turn == RED) {
     opponent= BLUE;
       }
   else {
     opponent= RED;
       }

   // For each move possibility,

   for(iterations= 0; iterations < 8; iterations++) {

      // Prepare ghost boards for shallow ply search.

      initialize_ghosts();

      // Transfer the data from the main game board to
      // a ghost board.

      copy_board_to_ghost1();

      // Determine the number of pieces in each column.

      number=
         number_of_squares_in_ghost1_column((UCHAR)iterations);

      // If the column is filled with 9 pieces then a move in the
      // column will be illegal. Placing a 1 in a coffin[] array element
      // tells Dr. Plopper to avoid making a move in that column.

      if(number == 8) {
         coffin[iterations]= 1;
            }
```

6.3 THE create_coffin(turn) FUNCTION

```
        // If a legal move is possible, check and see what
        // may happen.

        if (number < 8) {

           // Place a move on the phantom board.

           ghost1[7 - number][iterations]= turn;

           // If the human will have a winning move, then
           // make sure Dr. Plopper doesn't make a move
           // in this column.

           if(ghost1_coffin(turn)) {
              coffin[iterations]= 1;
              }
           }

        // Here is a search of a potential human fork:

        if ((number < 7) && (!coffin[iterations])) {

           // Place Dr. Plopper's first ply move.

           ghost1[7 - number][iterations]= turn;

           // Place the human's second ply move directly above
           // Dr. Plopper's move.

           ghost1[6 - number][iterations]= opponent;

           // if the human will have two or more winning
           // possibilities then make sure that Dr. Plopper
           // avoids making this move

           result= search_ghost1_fork_move(opponent);

           if(result >= 2) {
              coffin[iterations]= 1;
              }
           }
        }
} ∎
```

6.4 The `create_coffin_o(opponent)` function

The `create_coffin_o(...)` function places a 2 into elements of the `coffin[]` array, indicating that a given column would be a bad place for the human to move. The overall strategy here is to maximize the bad move opportunities for the human. Listing 6.5 presents the source code for `create_coffin_o(...)`.

❑ **Listing 6.5** Source code for the `create_coffin_o(...)` function.

```
/////////////////////////////////////
//
// Bad moves for the human to make.
//

void create_coffin_o(UCHAR opponent)
{
UCHAR number;
UCHAR priority[8];
int   iterations, iterations1, iterations2;
UCHAR move;
UCHAR turn;
UCHAR row, result;

   if(opponent == RED) {
      turn= BLUE;
      }
   else {
      turn= RED;
      }

   // For each move possibility,

   for(iterations= 0; iterations < 8; iterations++) {

      // Prepare ghost boards for shallow ply search.

      initialize_ghosts();

      // Transfer the data from the main game board to
      // a ghost board.

      copy_board_to_ghost1();
```

6.4 THE create_coffin_o(opponent) FUNCTION

```
      // Determine the number of pieces in each column.

      number=
         number_of_squares_in_ghost1_column((UCHAR)iterations);

      // If the column is filled with 9 pieces, then a move in the
      // column will be illegal. Placing a 1 in a coffin[] array element
      // tells Dr. Plopper to avoid making a move in that column.

      if(number == 8) {
         coffin[iterations]= 1;
         }

      // If a legal move is possible, check and see what
      // may happen.

      if (number < 8) {

         // Place a move on the phantom board.

         ghost1[7 - number][iterations]= opponent;

         // If the human will have a winning move, then
         // make sure Dr. Plopper doesn't make a move
         // in this column.

         if((ghost1_coffin(opponent)) && (!coffin[iterations])) {
             coffin[iterations]= 2;
            }
         }

    // Here is a search of a potential Dr. Plopper fork:

   if ((number < 7) && (!coffin[iterations])) {

         // Place human's first ply move.

         ghost1[7 - number][iterations]= opponent;

         // Place Dr. Plopper's second ply move directly above
         // Dr. Plopper's move

         ghost1[6 - number][iterations]= turn;
```

```
            // If Dr. Plopper will have two or more winning
            // possibilities, then make sure that Dr. Plopper
            // avoids making this move -- and let's hope that
            // the human makes this move.

            result= search_ghost1_fork_move(turn);
            if(result >= 2) {
               coffin[iterations]= 2;
               }
            }
         }
      }
   } ■
```

6.5 The `create_win_board()` function

Listing 6.6 presents the source code for the `create_win_board(...)` function. This simple function uses an 8 × 8 array to hold information regarding win possibilities. One of four values may be placed in an element of the `win_board` array. A 0 signifies that if a piece were to eventually occupy that game board location, neither side would have a win. The three other possibilities are: the human would win, Dr. Plopper would win, or the human and Dr. Plopper would win.

❏ **Listing 6.6** Source code for the `create_win_board(...)` function.

```
//////////////////////////////////////
//
// Find potential win positions.
//

void create_win_board()
{
int    row, col;
UCHAR result;
```

```
            for(row=0; row < 8; row++) {
               for(col=0; col < 8; col++) {
                  win_board[row][col]= 0;
                  if(board[row][col] == 0) {
                     copy_board_to_ghost1();
                     ghost1[row][col]= RED;
                     result= search_ghost1();
                     if (result == RED) {
                        win_board[row][col]=RED;
                     }
                     copy_board_to_ghost1();
                     ghost1[row][col]= BLUE;
                     result= search_ghost1();
                     if((result == BLUE) && (win_board[row][col] == RED)) {
                         win_board[row][col]= RED_AND_BLUE;
                     }
                     if((result == BLUE) && (!win_board[row][col])) {
                         win_board[row][col]= BLUE;
                     }
                  }
               }
            }
         } ■
```

6.6 The coffin_pattern(turn) *function*

The coffin_pattern(...) function places a value of 3 or 4 into the appropriate element of the coffin[] array when it determines that making a move in that column would facilitate the creation of an advantageous vertical double win pattern for the human. Listing 6.7 presents the source code for the coffin_pattern(...) function.

❏ **Listing 6.7** Source code for the coffin_pattern(...) function.

```
////////////////////////////////////////////
//
// Initialize coffin with pattern information.
//
```

```
void coffin_pattern(UCHAR turn)
{
UCHAR iterations, iterations1;
UCHAR row, col, number, opponent;
UCHAR val1, val2;

   if(turn == RED) {
      opponent= BLUE;
      }
   else {
      opponent= RED;
      }

   for(iterations= 0; iterations < 8; iterations++) {
      copy_board_to_ghost1();
      val1= count_double_ghost1(opponent);
      number= number_of_squares_in_ghost1_column(iterations);
      if(number < 7) {
         ghost1[7 - number][iterations]= turn;
         ghost1[7 - number - 1][iterations]= opponent;
         create_win_ghost1();
         val2= count_double_ghost1(opponent);
         if ((coffin[iterations] != 1) && (val2 > val1)) {
           coffin[iterations]= 3;
           }
         }
      }

   for(iterations= 0; iterations < 8; iterations++) {
      copy_board_to_ghost1();
      val1= count_double_ghost1(turn);
      number= number_of_squares_in_ghost1_column(iterations);
      if(number < 7) {
         ghost1[7 - number][iterations]= opponent;
         ghost1[7 - number - 1][iterations]= turn;
         create_win_ghost1();
         val2= count_double_ghost1(turn);
         if ((coffin[iterations] != 1) && (coffin[iterations] != 2)
                              && (val2 > val1)) {
           coffin[iterations]= 4;
           }
         }
      }
} ∎
```

6.7 The `coffin_corner( UCHAR turn )` *function*

The coffin_corner(...) function is an example of highly specialized program instinct. It returns a highly effective defensive move under specialized circumstances. Even though we always tried to write program instinct and program learning functions which would take into account the widest variety of board positions, we knew that there would come times when we would need to use specialized program instinct to fill holes in our more generalized routines. The coffin_corner(...) function is such an example. Listing 6.8 presents its source code.

❏ **Listing 6.8** Source code for the coffin_corner(...) function.

```
////////////////////////////////////////////////////////
//
// Initialize coffin in specialized corner circumstance.
// Very defensive, and effective under many circumstances.
//
void coffin_corner(UCHAR turn)
{
UCHAR opponent;

   if(turn == RED) {
      opponent= BLUE;
      }
   else {
      opponent= RED;
      }

   if((board[7][0] == opponent) &&
      (!board[7][1])) {
         if(!coffin[1]) {
            coffin[1]= 2;
            }
         }

   if((board[7][7] == opponent) &&
      (!board[7][6])) {
         if(!coffin[6]) {
            coffin[6]= 2;
            }
         }
}
```

6.8 Summary

This source-code laden chapter carefully presents the implementation of the program instinct–related functions which evaluate the board and fill the `coffin[]` and `win_board[]` arrays at the very beginning of Dr. Plopper's move generation sequence.

The `coffin[]` array alerts Dr. Plopper to potentially weak moves which would not be detected by non-ply– and nonlearning-based program instinct moves. If a 0 is held in an element of the `coffin[]` array, it indicates that nothing unfortunate should happen if Dr. Plopper, at some later time in the move decision evaluation sequence, decides to move there. If a 1 appears in an element, it means that Dr. Plopper should move there to avoid a loss. If a 2 appears, it means that the move would be a weak move for the human opponent. Dr. Plopper doesn't want to eliminate a possibility for the human to make a weak move. If a 3 appears in an element, it means that if Dr. Plopper moves there s/he will be enhancing the chances for the human to create a double vertical win positional possibility. If a 4 appears in an element, it means that the human would create a double win for Dr. Plopper if s/he moves there.

chapter 7

Drop Four program instinct: Move decision scheme

This chapter discusses program instinct from a decision-making format. There are times when all programmers are faced with mutually exclusive goals. A classic example of this is program performance versus program size. In the case of designing Drop Four's program instinct, we knew that we'd be facing just that problem. In a protected mode programming environment such as OS/2, memory constraints are very loose, so performance always wins out. When programming in a real mode DOS environment, memory management can become a critical issue.

Using the OAI Paradigm as our guide we knew what we'd have to struggle to program Dr. Plopper so that s/he would be able to make move decisions in a timely fashion. That being our first priority, Narendra volunteered to open up his personal Drop Four decision making scheme. Following Narendra's lead, we developed the function `get_computer_move_first(...)`. This function is called when Dr. Plopper moves first. The `get_computer_move(...)` function is called when Dr. Plopper moves second.

7.1 The `get_computer_move_first(...)` *function*

The `get_computer_move_first(...)` function contains the logic which allows Dr. Plopper to move in a very rapid fashion (under 5 seconds on a 486 33-MHz computer) under all circumstances. Following Narendra's strategies, we decided to write functions which perform highly specialized tasks. For example, Narendra's first consideration involved making a move which would win the game if possible. This function requires a 1-ply search, which uses very little computer time. We knew that some of the other ply searches and the program subconscious marker matching functions would take more time than the 1-ply win search.

Our reasoning led us to follow the design strategy of coding short and separate functions which would return a move if one were available based on the requirements of the function. Under most circumstances, we tried to evaluate information based only on the move to be considered. While there might be thirty factors which go into selecting a move, all of them need not be considered, if the most desirable move is obvious. Choosing this path led us to write highly specialized move generation functions. Concentrating on having Dr. Plopper generate moves in a timely fashion pushed us to not think about code size.

This version of `get_computer_move_first(...)` supports four levels of play: new beginner, beginner, intermediate, and advanced. As you carefully review the code for this function it will be very easy for you to see which move generation functions are associated with each of the levels of play. Note that adding and deleting features from levels of play would prove to be quite a trivial coding task.

The decisions that go into making moves at the four levels of game play currently supported by Dr. Plopper are addressed in the next few paragraphs. Note that each entry in a table represents one consideration for a making a move. If the conditions for that consideration are met then the move is made and no other considerations are evaluated.

New beginner level

Dr. Plopper's decision-making structure at the new beginner playing level:

1. Report if the game is drawn or worst-case `coffin[]` move
2. Return a random move.

Beginner level

At the beginner level of play, Dr. Plopper forces the human to think of creating multiple winning possibilities, by blocking simple winning strategies. Eventually, the human will learn to create forks and vertical double win positions. The decision-making scheme for the beginner level of game play:

1. If human can win, block the win
2. Program instinct makes defensive move

7.1 THE get_computer_move_first(...) FUNCTION

3. Report if the game is drawn or worst-case coffin[] move
4. Return a random move.

Intermediate level

At the intermediate level of play, Dr. Plopper uses program instinct to play more aggressively, with a deeper arsenal of defensive maneuvers. Humans will be able to beat Dr. Plopper on the advanced level only if they can beat her/him on a regular basis on the intermediate level. The decision-making scheme for the intermediate level of game play:

1. If Dr. Plopper can win, make the winning move
2. If the human can win, block the win
3. Program instinct seeks to develop patterns if available
4. Program instinct makes a move via a general board evaluator
5. Report if the game is drawn or worst-case coffin[] move
6. Return a random move.

Advanced level

At the advanced level of game play, program learning kicks into gear. At the beginning of advanced level play, program instinct generates all the moves. Once Dr. Plopper loses a game, it will be analyzed and information from the loss will be integrated into future games. This is accomplished by saving the program subconscious to disk when the human quits to DOS. The section of the program subconscious which is saved to disk is automatically loaded immediately after Drop Four's program launch has been completed. This process is automatic and invisible to the user. The decision-making scheme for the advanced level of game play:

1. If Dr. Plopper can win, make the winning move
2. If the human can win, block the win
3. Program learning alters play to avoid previous loss (level 1)
4. Program learning alters play to avoid previous loss (level 2)
5. Program instinct creates fork
6. Program instinct creates fork after 2 ply
7. Program instinct defeats human fork
8. Program instinct defeats fork after 2 ply
9. Program instinct increases win possibilities on game board
10. Program learning uses winning human patterns against human
11. Program instinct creates double vertical wins

12. Program instinct creates winning patterns in 2 ply
13. Program learning markers defeat human's winning pattern (Level 4)
14. Program learning markers defeat human's winning pattern (Level 3)
15. Program instinct makes a move via a general board evaluator
16. Report if the game is drawn or worst-case `coffin[]` move
17. Return a random move.

Listing 7.1 presents the source code for the `get_computer_move_first(...)` function. This function is contained in `engine.c` and returns the move. In Drop Four's DOS character mode version this function is called from function `start_game(...)`.

❑ **Listing 7.1** Source code for the `get_computer_move_first(...)` function.

```
UCHAR get_computer_move_first( UCHAR game_difficulty,
                               UCHAR turn )
{
UCHAR number;
UCHAR win1[8][8];
UCHAR priority[8];
int   ctr;
int   iterations;
UCHAR move, opponent;

   move_counter++;

   // Set opponent.

   if( turn == RED ) {
      opponent= BLUE;
      }
   else {
      opponent= RED;
      }

   // Initialize column number array.

   for( iterations= 0; iterations < 8; iterations++ ) {
      move= number_of_squares_in_column( ( UCHAR )iterations );
      squares[iterations]=
           number_of_squares_in_column( ( UCHAR )iterations );
      }
```

7.1 THE get_computer_move_first(...) FUNCTION

```
// Initialize the coffin[] array, initiate
// a preliminary evaluation of the game board,
// and place the results in the coffin[] array.

init_coffin();
create_coffin( turn );
create_coffin_o( opponent );
create_win_board();
evaluate_board( turn, FIRST );
coffin_pattern( turn );

// The second player will be human
// if Dr. Plopper moves first.

if ( second_player==HUMAN ) {
  opponent_type_move( opponent );
  }
else {
  opponent_type_move_comp( opponent );
  }

// Put information in end_game_list
// if there is a human player or
// if it's the first/second move.

if ( moves_offset == 0 ) {
  end_game_list[moves_offset]= 9;
  }
else {
  if ( second_player == HUMAN ) {

    }
  }

if ( ( moves_offset==0 ) && ( !first_sequence_flag ) ) {
    move= generate_first_move();

    // If the debugging flag is set,
    // send this information to the
    // screen.

    if( debugging ) {
       report_move( "first_move  " );
       }
```

```
      // Record the move type in program subconscious.

      move_type[moves_offset]= 0;
      return move;
   }

   // On beginner level, simply generate
   // a random move.

   if( game_difficulty == NEW_BEGINNER ) {

      // At the new beginner level Dr. Plopper
      // checks, and makes a random move
      // if the game has not been drawn.

      move= is_coffined_out();

      // If all the elements in the coffin
      // array have been filled with values
      // greater than 0 but the game has not
      // been drawn.

      if( move < 8 ) {

         // If the debugging flag is set,
         // display the debugging information
         // on the screen.

         if( debugging ) {
            report_move( "no_moves    " );
         }

         return move;
      }

      // If the debugging flag is set,
      // send this information to the
      // screen.

      if( debugging ) {
         report_move( "random      " );
      }
```

7.1 THE get_computer_move_first(...) FUNCTION

```
      // If the is_coffined_out(...) function
      // does not return a legal move, then
      // a random legal move will be generated.

      return( ( UCHAR )do_random_move() );
   }

   // Things become more difficult at the
   // beginner level.

   if( game_difficulty == BEGINNER ) {

      // Block a loss if possible.

      move= check_for_loss( turn );

      if( move == NO_IMMEDIATE_LOSS ) {

         // If there is no immediate loss, then
         // generate a move from program instinct.
         // A defensive (instinctive pattern
         // disruption) is invoked.

         move= opening_book_defense( turn );

         if( ( move != NO_BOOK_MOVE ) &&
             ( move < 8 )              &&
             ( move >= 0 ) ) {

            // If the debugging flag is set,
            // send this information to the
            // screen.

            if( debugging ) {
               report_move( "opening_book" );
            }

            return move;
         }

         // No good moves have been found via
         // program instinct, and the best of
         // what's available in the coffin[]
         // array is selected.
```

```
      move= is_coffined_out();

      if( move < 8 ) {

         // If the debugging flag is set,
         // send this information to the
         // screen.

         if( debugging ) {
            report_move( "no_moves    " );
            }

         return move;
         }

      // If the debugging flag is set,
      // send this information to the
      // screen.

      if( debugging ) {
         report_move( "random      " );
         }

      // Program instinct has not produced
      // a move, so Dr. Plopper closes her/his
      // eyes and makes a random selection.

      return( ( UCHAR )do_random_move() );
      }

   else {

      // If the debugging flag is set,
      // send this information to the
      // screen.

      if( debugging ) {
         report_move( "check_loss  " );
         }

      return( move );
      }
}
```

7.1 THE get_computer_move_first(...) FUNCTION

```
// Things become considerably more difficult
// for the human player at the intermediate
// level.

if( game_difficulty == INTERMEDIATE ) {

   // If Dr. Plopper can win, make the
   // winning move now. This program instinct-
   // generated move is based on a 1-ply
   // search with a specific goal. It's very
   // fast and deadly accurate.

   move= check_for_win( turn );

   if( move != NO_IMMEDIATE_WIN ) {

      // If the debugging flag is set,
      // send this information to the
      // screen.

      if( debugging ) {
         report_move( "check_win    " );
         }

      // Record the move type in program subconscious.

      move_type[moves_offset]= 1;

      // Make the winning move.

      return move;
      }

   // Determine if Dr. Plopper must block
   // a potential human win.

   move= check_for_loss( turn );

   if( move == NO_IMMEDIATE_LOSS ) {
```

```
   // Dr. Plopper did not need to make
   // an immediate move to prevent a loss
   // to the human, so additional information
   // is added to the coffin[] array. That
   // happens at this juncture as implementation
   // of the OAI paradigm's thrust at making
   // moves in a human time frame. The information
   // added to the coffin[] array at this juncture
   // need not be determined if the Dr. needed
   // to immediately block a human win.

   coffin_pattern( turn );

   // At this point, Dr. Plopper is turning
   // to program instinct to try to slowly
   // build patterns which would prove
   // advantageous to her/his position.
   // Here program instinct is used to
   // generate an offensive move.

   move= check_for_pattern( turn );

   if( move != NO_PATTERN_DETECTED ) {

      // If the debugging flag is set,
      // send this information to the
      // screen.

      if( debugging ) {
         report_move( "OFF pattern " );
         }

      // Record the move type in program subconscious.

      move_type[moves_offset]= 2;
      return move;
      }

   // At this point, Dr. Plopper is turning
   // to program instinct to try to slowly
   // build patterns which would prove
   // advantageous to her/his position.
   // Here program instinct is used to
   // generate an defensive move.
```

7.1 THE get_computer_move_first(...) FUNCTION

```
            move= check_for_pattern( opponent );

         if( move != NO_PATTERN_DETECTED ) {

            // If the debugging flag is set,
            // send this information to the
            // screen.

            if( debugging ) {
               report_move( "DEF pattern  " );
               }

            // Record the move type in program subconscious.

            move_type[moves_offset]= 2;
            return move;
            }

         // If a move has not been generated at this
         // point in the move generation scheme, then
         // the general positional evaluation function
         // is called. In a sense, this function
         // sees the board as a "gestalt" whole,
         // and uses much of program instinct to
         // generate a sensible move. It's a quiet
         // and sound function.

         move= first_ply_move( turn, first_all );

         if( move != NO_FIRST_PLY_MOVE ) {

            // If the debugging flag is set,
            // send this information to the
            // screen.

            if( debugging ) {
              report_move( "first_ply  " );
              }
```

```
            // Record the move type in program subconscious.

            move_type[moves_offset]= 0;
            return move;
        }

    }

    else {

        // Record win-blocking move
        // in program subconscious,

        move_type[moves_offset]= 1;

        // and make the saving move.

        return( move );
    }

    // If the general positional evaluation
    // has failed to generate a move then
    // a less comprehensive program instinct
    // pattern creation function will try
    // to generate the move.

    move= do_positional_move( turn );

    if( move < 8 ) {

        // Record the move type in program subconscious.

        move_type[moves_offset]= 0;
        return( move );
    }

    // No good moves have been found via
    // program instinct, and the best of
    // what's available in the coffin[]
    // array is selected.

    move= is_coffined_out();

    if( move < 8 ) {
```

7.1 THE get_computer_move_first(...) FUNCTION

```
         // Record the move type in program
         // subconscious.

         move_type[moves_offset]= 0;
         return move;
      }

      // Record the move type in program
      // subconscious.

      move_type[moves_offset]= 0;

      // Dr. Plopper closes his/her eyes
      // and randomly selects a move.

      return( ( UCHAR )do_random_move() );

   }

   // At the ADVANCED level of play, Dr. Plopper
   // is finally allowed to show his powerful
   // capacity to learn from her/his mistakes
   // and demonstrate learning by avoiding the
   // moves which led to a previously experienced
   // loss. The more Dr. Plopper loses, the smarter
   // s/he becomes. The increase in Dr. Plopper's
   // skills become noticeable in orders of magnitude.
   // Quite cool.

   if( game_difficulty == ADVANCED ) {

      // Once again, supporting a quick response.
      // Dr. Plopper need not consider seeing if
      // s/he can win before the s/he gets a few
      // moves under her/his belt.

      if ( moves_offset > 5 ) {

         // If Dr. Plopper can win, make the
         // winning move now. This program instinct-
         // generated move is based on a 1-ply
         // search with a specific goal. It's very
         // fast and deadly accurate.
```

```
            move= check_for_win( turn );

         if( move != NO_IMMEDIATE_WIN ) {

            // If the debugging flag is set,
            // send this information to the screen.

            if( debugging ) {
               report_move( "check_win        " );
               }

            // Record the move type in program subconscious.

            move_type[moves_offset]= 1;

             return move;
            }
         }

      if ( moves_offset > 5 ) {

         // If Dr. Plopper will lose, make the block move
         // now. This program instinct-generated move is
         // based on a 1-ply search with a specific goal.
         // It's very fast and deadly accurate.

         move= check_for_loss( turn );

         if( move != NO_IMMEDIATE_LOSS ) {

            // if the debugging flag is set, send this
            // information to the screen.

            if( debugging ) {
               report_move( "check_loss  " );
               }

            // Record the move type in program subconscious.

            move_type[moves_offset]= 1;
            return( move );

            }
         }
```

7.1 THE get_computer_move_first(...) FUNCTION

```
    if ( moves_offset > 1 ) {

      // Program learning kicks into action here.
      // The forced move algorithm is used to see if
      // a loss has been previously experienced. Dr.
      // Plopper searches through program subconscious
      // to find a memory of a level-one match.

      move= off_first_move_check( moves_offset );

      if( move != NO_MATCHING_RECORD ) {

         // If the debugging flag is set,
         // send this information to the
         // screen.

         if( debugging ) {
            report_move( "first_analys" );
            }

         // Record the move type in program
         // subconscious.

         move_type[moves_offset]= 3;
          return move;
         }
      }

   if ( moves_offset > 1 ) {

      // Program learning kicks into action here.
      // The forced move algorithm is used to see if
      // a loss has been previously experienced. Dr.
      // Plopper searches through program subconscious
      // to find a memory of a level-two match.

      move= off_second_move_check( moves_offset );

      if( move != NO_MATCHING_RECORD ) {

         // if the debugging flag is set,
         // send this information to the
         // screen.
```

```
            if( debugging ) {
               report_move( "2nd_analys  " );
            }

            // Record the move type in program
            // subconscious.

            move_type[moves_offset]= 3;
             return move;
            }
      }

   if ( moves_offset > 3 ) {

         // Program instinct here seeks
         // to find a 2-ply fork.

         move= look_ahead( turn );

         if( move != NO_FORK_FOUND ) {

            // If the debugging flag is set,
            // send this information to the
            // screen.

            if( debugging ) {
               report_move( "look_ahead  " );
            }

            // Record the move type in program
            // subconscious.

            move_type[moves_offset]= 1;

            return move;
            }
      }

   if ( moves_offset > 3 ) {

         // Program instinct seeks to create
         // a forced win for Dr. Plopper in
         // two moves. This is an offensive
         // strategy.
```

7.1 THE get_computer_move_first(...) FUNCTION

```
         move= create_setup2( turn );

      if( move != NO_SETUP_FOUND ) {

         // If the debugging flag is set,
         // send this information to the screen.

         if( debugging ) {
            report_move( "creat_setup2 " );
            }

         // Record the move type in program subconscious.

         move_type[moves_offset]= 1;

         return move;
         }
      }

   if ( moves_offset > 5 ) {

      // Program instinct seeks to stop
      // a forced win for the human in
      // two moves. This is a defensive
      // strategy.

      move= stop_setup2( turn );

      if( move != NO_SETUP_FOUND ) {

         // if the debugging flag is set, send this
         // information to the screen.

         if( debugging ) {
            report_move( "stop_setup2 " );
            }

         // Record the move type in program subconscious.

         move_type[moves_offset]= 1;

         return move;
         }
      }
```

```
    if ( moves_offset > 5 ) {

       // Program instinct seeks to find
       // an impending 2-ply fork via ply
       // searching, and will block its
       // formation if found. This is a defensive
       // strategy.

       move= look_ahead_opp( opponent );

       if( move != NO_FORK_FOUND ) {

          // If the debugging flag is set,
          // send this information to the
          // screen.

          if( debugging ) {
             report_move( "lk_ahead_opp" );
             }

          // Record the move type in program
          // subconscious.

          move_type[moves_offset]= 1;

          return move;
          }
       }

    if ( moves_offset > 9 ) {

       // Program instinct seeks to discover
       // how many "forced win" squares there
       // will be on the board after the 1-
       // ply move. The theory is that the
       // greater the number of winning
       // possiblities Dr. Plopper will have
       // on the game board, the better her/his
       // position will be.

       move= forced_win_board( turn );

       if( move != NO_ADVANTAGE ) {
```

7.1 THE get_computer_move_first(...) FUNCTION

```
            // If the debugging flag is set,
            // send this information to the
            // screen.

            if( debugging ) {
               report_move( "forced_win_b  " );
            }

            // Record the move type in program
            // subconscious.

            move_type[moves_offset]= 1;

            return move;
            }
      }

   if ( moves_offset > 5 ) {

      // Program learning searches program
      // subconscious to find a first-level
      // record of moves when Dr. Plopper
      // made the first move of the game.
      // If Dr. Plopper recognizes that the
      // sequence of moves in the program
      // subconscious matches the sequence
      // of moves currently being played,
      // s/he plays the "trap" move which
      // a human has previously used against
      // her/him. This is an offensive
      // strategy.

      move= first_human_win( moves_offset );

      if( move != NO_HUMAN_WIN ) {

         // If the debugging flag is set,
         // send this information to the
         // screen.

         if( debugging ) {
            report_move( "first_human " );
         }
```

```
         // Record the move type in program
         // subconscious.

         move_type[moves_offset]= 5;

         return move;
         }
      }

   if ( moves_offset > 5 ) {

      // Program learning searches the program
      // subconscious to find a second-level
      // record of moves when Dr. Plopper
      // made the first move of the game.
      // If Dr. Plopper recognizes that the
      // sequence of moves in the program
      // subconscious matches the sequence
      // of moves currently being played,
      // s/he plays the "trap" move which
      // a human has previously used against
      // her/him. This is an offensive
      // strategy.

      move= second_human_win( moves_offset );

      if( move != NO_HUMAN_WIN ) {

         // If the debugging flag is set,
         // send this information to the
         // screen.

         if( debugging ) {
            report_move( "second_human" );
            }

         // Record the move type in program
         // subconscious.

         move_type[moves_offset]= 5;

         return move;
         }
      }
```

7.1 THE get_computer_move_first(...) FUNCTION

```
   if ( moves_offset > 7 ) {

      // Program instinct seeks to create
      // a vertical double win pattern
      // for Dr. Plopper. This is a ply
      // search based move which proves very
      // fast and deadly. It is an offensive
      // move.

      move= create_double_pattern( turn );

      if( move != NO_DOUBLE_PATTERN ) {

         // If the debugging flag is set,
         // send this information to the
         // screen.

         if( debugging ) {
            report_move( "create_2_pat  " );
            }

         // Record the move type in program
         // subconscious.

         move_type[moves_offset]= 1;

         return move;
         }
      }

   if ( moves_offset > 7 ) {

      // Program instinct seeks to defeat
      // a vertical double win pattern
      // for the human. This is a ply
      // search based move which proves very
      // effective. It is a defensive move.

      move= create_double_pattern( opponent );

      if( move != NO_DOUBLE_PATTERN ) {
```

```
         // If the debugging flag is set,
         // send this information to the
         // screen.

         if( debugging ) {
            report_move( "stop_2_pat  " );
         }

         // Record the move type in program
         // subconscious.

         move_type[moves_offset]= 1;

         return move;
      }
   }

   if ( moves_offset > 7 ) {

      // Program instinct uses ply searching
      // to create a double win pattern in
      // two ply. It's a quick and effective
      // offensive strategy.

      move= create_setup_2pat( turn );

      if( move != NO_SETUP_FOUND ) {

         // If the debugging flag is set,
         // send this information to the
         // screen.

         if( debugging ) {
            report_move( "setup_2_pat " );
         }

         // Record the move type in program
         // subconscious.

         move_type[moves_offset]= 1;

         return move;
      }
   }
```

7.1 THE get_computer_move_first(...) FUNCTION

```
      if ( moves_offset > 7 ) {

         // Program instinct uses ply searching
         // to defeat a double win pattern in
         // two ply. It's a quick and effective
         // defensive strategy.

         move= stop_setup_2pat( turn );

         if( move != NO_SETUP_FOUND ) {

            // If the debugging flag is set,
            // send this information to the screen.

            if( debugging ) {
               report_move( "o_setup_2pat" );
               }

            // Record the move type in program subconscious.

            move_type[moves_offset]= 1;

            return move;
            }
         }

      if ( first_sequence_flag == 1 ) {

         // Program learning continues an opening
         // sequence of moves if this portion of
         // the move selection function has
         // been reached.

         move= first_openings( sequence, moves_offset );

         if( move != NO_MORE_SEQUENCE ) {

            // If the debugging flag is set,
            // send this information to the
            // screen.

            if( debugging ) {
               report_move( "sequence     " );
               }
```

```
            // Record the move type in program
            // subconscious.

            move_type[moves_offset]= 7;

            return move;
            }
         else {
            sequence= move;
            first_sequence_flag= 2;
            }
         }

      if ( moves_offset > 7 ) {

         // Program learning function seeks to search
         // the program subconscious until it finds
         // a marker with a pattern of turn's
         // pieces. It seeks to make a move to
         // enhance the development of the advantageous
         // marker. This is an offensive move.

         move= find_winning_pattern( turn, 4 );

         if( move != NO_WINNING_PATTERN ) {

            // If the debugging flag is set,
            // send this information to the
            // screen.

            if( debugging ) {
               report_move( "pat_ana_OFF4" );
               }

            // Record the move type in program
            // subconscious.

            move_type[moves_offset]= 4;

            return move;
            }
         }
```

7.1 THE get_computer_move_first(...) FUNCTION

```
      if ( moves_offset > 7 ) {

         // Program learning function seeks to search
         // the program subconscious until it finds
         // a marker with a pattern of turn's
         // pieces. It seeks to make a move to
         // disrupt the development of the advantageous
         // marker. This is an defensive move.

         move= find_winning_pattern( opponent, 4 );

         if( move != NO_WINNING_PATTERN ) {

            // If the debugging flag is set,
            // send this information to the
            // screen.

            if( debugging ) {
               report_move( "pat_ana_DEF4" );
               }

            // Record the move type in program
            // subconscious.

            move_type[moves_offset]= 4;

            return move;
            }
         }

      if ( moves_offset > 3 ) {

         // Program instinct uses a general
         // board evaluation function to
         // find a move which creates the
         // most advantageous patterns
         // for Dr. Plopper. It's a ply search
         // based function. It returns moves
         // with a  human feel.

         move= check_for_pattern( turn );

         if( move != NO_PATTERN_DETECTED ) {
```

```
         // If the debugging flag is set,
         // send this information to the
         // screen.

         if( debugging ) {
            report_move( "OFF pattern  " );
         }

         // Record the move type in program subconscious.

         move_type[moves_offset]= 2;

         return move;
         }
      }

   if ( moves_offset > 3 ) {

      // Program instinct uses a general
      // board evaluation function to
      // find a move which defeats the
      // most advantageous patterns
      // for the human. It's a ply search
      // based function. It returns moves
      // with a  human feel.

      move= check_for_pattern( opponent );

      if( move != NO_PATTERN_DETECTED ) {

         // If the debugging flag is set,
         // send this information to the screen.

         if( debugging ) {
            report_move( "DEF pattern  " );
         }

         // Record the move type in program subconscious.

         move_type[moves_offset]= 2;

         return move;
         }
      }
```

7.1 THE get_computer_move_first(...) FUNCTION

```
      if ( moves_offset > 5 ) {

         // Program learning function seeks to search
         // the program subconscious until it finds
         // a marker with a pattern of turn's
         // pieces. It seeks to make a move to
         // enhance the development of the advantageous
         // marker. This is an offensive move.

         move= find_winning_pattern( turn, 3 );

         if( move != NO_WINNING_PATTERN ) {

            // If the debugging flag is set,
            // send this information to the
            // screen.

            if( debugging ) {
               report_move( "pat_ana_OFF3" );
               }

            // Record the move type in program
            // subconscious.

            move_type[moves_offset]= 4;

            return move;
            }
         }

      if ( moves_offset > 5 ) {

         // Program learning function seeks to search
         // the program subconscious until it finds
         // a marker with a pattern of turn's
         // pieces. It seeks to make a move to
         // defeat the development of the advantageous
         // marker. This is a defensive move.

         move= find_winning_pattern( opponent, 3 );

         if( move != NO_WINNING_PATTERN ) {
```

```
            // If the debugging flag is set,
            // send this information to the
            // screen.

            if( debugging ) {
               report_move( "pat_ana_DEF3" );
               }

            // Record the move type in program
            // subconscious.

            move_type[moves_offset]= 4;

            return move;
            }
      }

   // If a move has not been generated at this
   // point in the move generation scheme, then
   // the general positional evaluation function
   // is called. In a sense, this function
   // sees the board as a "gestalt" whole,
   // and uses much of program instinct to
   // generate a sensible move. It's a quiet
   // and sound function.

   move= first_ply_move( turn, first_all );

   if( move != NO_FIRST_PLY_MOVE ) {

      // If the debugging flag is set,
      // send this information to the
      // screen.

      if( debugging ) {
         report_move( "first_ply " );
         }

      // Record the move type in program subconscious.

      move_type[moves_offset]= 0;

      return move;
      }
```

```
         // No good moves have been found via program instinct, and the
         // best of what's available in the coffin[] array is selected.

         move= is_coffined_out();

         if( move < 8 ) {

            if ( debugging ) {
              report_move( "mo moves    " );
              }

            // Record the move type in program subconscious.

            move_type[moves_offset]= 9;

            return move;
            }

         // If the debugging flag is set,
         // send this information to the screen.

         if( debugging ) {
           report_move( "randon   " );
            }

         // Record the move type in program subconscious.

         move_type[moves_offset]= 0;
         return( ( UCHAR )do_random_move() );

         }
   } ■
```

7.2 Summary

Move selection blends functions which implement both program instinct and program learning. The nature of the blend proves quite critical to both the quality of the move being selected and the time it takes to select that move. This chapter presented four tables which outlined the decision-making scheme on Drop Four's four game play levels. The source code implementation of the move selection criteria was presented in Listing 7.1.

chapter 8

Drop Four program instinct: Ply searching

This chapter focuses on how shallow-ply searches are used to facilitate program instinct. When we wrote these functions we were concentrating on implementing learning and never imagined that these lazily conceived "block-copied" routines would find their way into print. However, they work as billed, so they're in the book. But please understand that when we write the next iteration of this code it will look very, very different....

What follows are the data and source code used to manage ply searches. Ugly, but gets the job done.

8.1 Ply search data and functions

Listing 8.1 presents the source code for the program subconscious used in ply searching. The arrays are all 8 × 8 dimensioned unsigned characters.

❑ **Listing 8.1** Source code for the global board data.

```
/////////////////////////////////////
//
// Global boards.
```

```
UCHAR board[8][8]= {
                { 0, 0, 0, 0, 0, 0, 0, 0 },
                { 0, 0, 0, 0, 0, 0, 0, 0 },
                { 0, 0, 0, 0, 0, 0, 0, 0 },
                { 0, 0, 0, 0, 0, 0, 0, 0 },
                { 0, 0, 0, 0, 0, 0, 0, 0 },
                { 0, 0, 0, 0, 0, 0, 0, 0 },
                { 0, 0, 0, 0, 0, 0, 0, 0 },
                { 0, 0, 0, 0, 0, 0, 0, 0 }};

UCHAR win_board[8][8]= {
                { 0, 0, 0, 0, 0, 0, 0, 0 },
                { 0, 0, 0, 0, 0, 0, 0, 0 },
                { 0, 0, 0, 0, 0, 0, 0, 0 },
                { 0, 0, 0, 0, 0, 0, 0, 0 },
                { 0, 0, 0, 0, 0, 0, 0, 0 },
                { 0, 0, 0, 0, 0, 0, 0, 0 },
                { 0, 0, 0, 0, 0, 0, 0, 0 },
                { 0, 0, 0, 0, 0, 0, 0, 0 }};

/////////////////////////////////////
//
// Ghosts for think-a-head.
//

UCHAR ghost1[8][8]= {
                { 0, 0, 0, 0, 0, 0, 0, 0 },
                { 0, 0, 0, 0, 0, 0, 0, 0 },
                { 0, 0, 0, 0, 0, 0, 0, 0 },
                { 0, 0, 0, 0, 0, 0, 0, 0 },
                { 0, 0, 0, 0, 0, 0, 0, 0 },
                { 0, 0, 0, 0, 0, 0, 0, 0 },
                { 0, 0, 0, 0, 0, 0, 0, 0 },
                { 0, 0, 0, 0, 0, 0, 0, 0 }};

UCHAR ghost2[8][8]= {
                { 0, 0, 0, 0, 0, 0, 0, 0 },
                { 0, 0, 0, 0, 0, 0, 0, 0 },
                { 0, 0, 0, 0, 0, 0, 0, 0 },
                { 0, 0, 0, 0, 0, 0, 0, 0 },
                { 0, 0, 0, 0, 0, 0, 0, 0 },
                { 0, 0, 0, 0, 0, 0, 0, 0 },
                { 0, 0, 0, 0, 0, 0, 0, 0 },
                { 0, 0, 0, 0, 0, 0, 0, 0 }};
```

8.1 PLY SEARCH DATA AND FUNCTIONS

```
UCHAR ghost3[8][8]= {
                { 0, 0, 0, 0, 0, 0, 0, 0 },
                { 0, 0, 0, 0, 0, 0, 0, 0 },
                { 0, 0, 0, 0, 0, 0, 0, 0 },
                { 0, 0, 0, 0, 0, 0, 0, 0 },
                { 0, 0, 0, 0, 0, 0, 0, 0 },
                { 0, 0, 0, 0, 0, 0, 0, 0 },
                { 0, 0, 0, 0, 0, 0, 0, 0 },
                { 0, 0, 0, 0, 0, 0, 0, 0 }};

UCHAR ghost4[8][8]= {
                { 0, 0, 0, 0, 0, 0, 0, 0 },
                { 0, 0, 0, 0, 0, 0, 0, 0 },
                { 0, 0, 0, 0, 0, 0, 0, 0 },
                { 0, 0, 0, 0, 0, 0, 0, 0 },
                { 0, 0, 0, 0, 0, 0, 0, 0 },
                { 0, 0, 0, 0, 0, 0, 0, 0 },
                { 0, 0, 0, 0, 0, 0, 0, 0 },
                { 0, 0, 0, 0, 0, 0, 0, 0 }};

UCHAR ghost5[8][8]= {
                { 0, 0, 0, 0, 0, 0, 0, 0 },
                { 0, 0, 0, 0, 0, 0, 0, 0 },
                { 0, 0, 0, 0, 0, 0, 0, 0 },
                { 0, 0, 0, 0, 0, 0, 0, 0 },
                { 0, 0, 0, 0, 0, 0, 0, 0 },
                { 0, 0, 0, 0, 0, 0, 0, 0 },
                { 0, 0, 0, 0, 0, 0, 0, 0 },
                { 0, 0, 0, 0, 0, 0, 0, 0 }};

UCHAR ghost6[8][8]= {
                { 0, 0, 0, 0, 0, 0, 0, 0 },
                { 0, 0, 0, 0, 0, 0, 0, 0 },
                { 0, 0, 0, 0, 0, 0, 0, 0 },
                { 0, 0, 0, 0, 0, 0, 0, 0 },
                { 0, 0, 0, 0, 0, 0, 0, 0 },
                { 0, 0, 0, 0, 0, 0, 0, 0 },
                { 0, 0, 0, 0, 0, 0, 0, 0 },
                { 0, 0, 0, 0, 0, 0, 0, 0 }}; ∎
```

8.2 Initializing ghost boards

Listing 8.2 presents the sample source code for the initialization functions, which set the values of the ghost board array elements to 0. There is one function for each of the ghost arrays residing in the program subconscious.

❏ **Listing 8.2** Functions that initialize the ghost board arrays.

```
///////////////////////////////////////
//
// Initialize ghosts.
//

void initialize_ghosts()
{
int row, column;

   // Write 0s to array.

   for(row= 0; row < 8; row++) {
      for(column= 0; column < 8; column++) {
         ghost1[row][column]= 0;
         }
      }
} ■
```

8.3 Relocating data between ghost boards

Listing 8.3 presents a sample function which relocates data between the main game board and the ghost boards.

❏ **Listing 8.3** Functions that relocate data between game boards.

```
///////////////////////////////////////
//
// Copy the main board to ghost 1.
//
```

```
void copy_board_to_ghost1()
{
int row, column;

   // Transfer data.

   for(row= 0; row < 8; row++) {
      for(column= 0; column < 8; column++) {
         ghost1[row][column]= board[row][column];
         }
      }
} ■
```

8.4 Getting the number of pieces in a ghost column

Listing 8.4 presents the source code listing to a sample function which returns the number of pieces currently occupying squares in a column on the game board.

❏ **Listing 8.4** Functions that count the number of pieces in a game or ghost board column.

```
/////////////////////////////////////
//
// Return the number of squares in
// ghost1 column.
//

UCHAR number_of_squares_in_ghost1_column(UCHAR column)
{
UCHAR sum;
int   row;

   for(row= 0, sum= 0; row < 8; row++) {
      if(ghost1[row][column]) {
         sum+= 1;
         }
      }
   return sum;

} ■
```

8.5 Determining double wins on ghost boards

Double wins (forks) are very desirable patterns. If a player can create a situation for a double win, then her/his chances to win greatly increase. Listing 8.5 presents sample source code to a function which seeks to find double wins during ply searches.

❏ **Listing 8.5** Functions that seek double wins during ply searches.

```
/////////////////////////////////////
//
// How many double wins in ghost1?
//

UCHAR count_double_ghost1(UCHAR turn)
{
UCHAR row, col, opponent;
UCHAR number =0;

   if(turn == RED) {
      opponent= BLUE;
      }
   else {
      opponent= RED;
      }

   create_win_ghost1();

   for(col= 0; col < 8; col++) {
      for(row= 7; row > 0 ; row--) {
         if((win_ghost1[row - 1][col] == turn) &&
            (win_ghost1[row][col] == turn)) {
            number += 1;
            }
         if((win_ghost1[row - 1][col] == RED_AND_BLUE) &&
            (win_ghost1[row][col] == turn)) {
            number += 1;
            }
         }
      }

   return number;
} ∎
```

8.6 Determining wins on ghost boards

Listing 8.6 presents a sample function which seeks to determine if there are any potential wins on a ghost board. The idea is that the greater the ratio of potential Dr. Plopper wins to potential human wins, the better Dr. Plopper's position is.

❏ **Listing 8.6** Functions that find wins during ply searches.

```
/////////////////////////////////////
//
// How many wins and
// for whom in ghost1?
//

void create_win_ghost1()
{
int   row, col;
UCHAR result;

   for(row=0; row < 8; row++) {
      for(col=0; col < 8; col++) {
         win_ghost1[row][col]= 0;
         if(ghost1[row][col] == 0) {
            copy_ghost1_to_ghost2();
            ghost2[row][col]= RED;
            result= search_ghost2();
            if (result == RED) {
              win_ghost1[row][col]=RED;
              }
            copy_ghost1_to_ghost2();
            ghost2[row][col]= BLUE;
            result= search_ghost2();
            if((result == BLUE) && (win_ghost1[row][col] == RED)) {
              win_ghost1[row][col]= RED_AND_BLUE;
              }
            if((result == BLUE) && (!win_ghost1[row][col])) {
              win_ghost1[row][col]= BLUE;
              }
            }
         }
      }
} ■
```

8.7 Searching for winning positions in ghost boards

Listing 8.7 presents a function which finds four-in-a-row wins on the game or ghost boards.

❑ **Listing 8.7**   Functions that find four-in-a-row wins on game or ghost boards.

```
//////////////////////////////////
//
// Search for 4 in a row in ghost1.

int search_ghost1()
{
int row,
    column,
    color= 0,
    count,
    temp_row,
    temp_col,
    ctr;

    for(row= 0; row < 8; row++) {
       for(column= 0; column < 8; column++) {
          if(ghost1[row][column]) {
             color = ghost1[row][column];

             // Check North.

             if(row >= 3) {
                temp_row= row - 1;
                temp_col= column;
                count= 1;
                for(ctr= 0; ctr < 3; ctr++) {
                   if(ghost1[temp_row--][temp_col] == color) {
                      count+= 1;
                   }
                   else {
                      break;
                   }
                   if (count == 4) {
                      return color;
                   }
                }
             }
```

8.7 SEARCHING FOR WINNING POSITIONS IN GHOST BOARDS

```
      // Check Northeast.

      if((row >= 3) && (column <= 4)) {
         temp_row= row - 1;
         temp_col= column + 1;
         count= 1;
          for(ctr= 0; ctr < 3; ctr++) {
            if(ghost1[temp_row--][temp_col++] == color) {
               count+= 1;
            }
            else {
               break;
            }
            if (count == 4) {
               return color;
            }
         }
      }

      // Check East.

      if(column <= 4) {
         temp_row= row;
         temp_col= column + 1;
         count= 1;
         for(ctr= 0; ctr < 3; ctr++) {
            if(ghost1[temp_row][temp_col++] == color) {
               count+= 1;
            }
            else {
               break;
            }
            if (count == 4) {
               return color;
            }
         }
      }
```

```
            // Check Southeast.

            if((row <= 4) && (column <= 4)) {
               temp_row= row + 1;
               temp_col= column + 1;
               count= 1;
               for(ctr= 0; ctr < 3; ctr++) {
                  if(ghost1[temp_row++][temp_col++] == color) {
                     count+= 1;
                  }
                  else {
                     break;
                  }
                  if (count == 4) {
                     return color;
                  }
               }
            }
         }
      }
   }
   return 0;
} ■
```

8.8 Can Dr. Plopper win on the next move?

This function looks one ply ahead to see if Dr. Plopper can make a winning move the next turn. If found, it returns the winning move. It's fast and lethal. The source code for the function check_for_win(...) is presented in Listing 8.8.

❑ **Listing 8.8** Source code for the check_for_win(...) function.

```
/////////////////////////////////////
//
// Make winning move if possible.
//

UCHAR check_for_win(UCHAR turn)
{
UCHAR number;
UCHAR squares[8];
UCHAR win1[8][8];
```

```
    UCHAR move_list[8];
    UCHAR priority[8];
    int   ctr;
    int   iterations;
    UCHAR opponent;
    UCHAR move;

       // Initialize move list with loss.

       for(iterations= 0; iterations < 8; iterations++) {
          initialize_ghosts();
          copy_board_to_ghost1();
          number= number_of_squares_in_ghost1_column((UCHAR)iterations);
          if(number == 8) {
             move_list[iterations]= 0;
             }
          else {
             ghost1[8 - number - 1][iterations]= turn;
             move_list[iterations]= search_ghost1();
             }
          }

       ////////////////////////////
       // Return immediately on
       // win.

       for(ctr= 0; ctr < 8; ctr++) {
          if((move_list[ctr] == turn) ) {
             return ctr;
             }
          }

       return NO_IMMEDIATE_WIN;
    } ■
```

8.9 Will Dr. Plopper have to block a human win?

This function looks one ply ahead to see if Dr. Plopper can block a potential win for the human this turn. If found, it returns the game-saving move. It's fast. The source code for the function `check_for_loss(...)` is presented in Listing 8.9.

❑ **Listing 8.9** Source code for the `check_for_loss(...)` function.

```
//////////////////////////////////////
//
// Block a loss if possible.
//

UCHAR check_for_loss(UCHAR turn)
{
UCHAR number;
UCHAR squares[8];
UCHAR win1[8][8];
UCHAR move_list[8];
UCHAR priority[8];
int   ctr;
int   iterations;
UCHAR opponent;
UCHAR move;

   if(turn == RED) {
      opponent= BLUE;
      }
   else {
      opponent= RED;
      }

   // Initialize move list with loss.

   for(iterations= 0; iterations < 8; iterations++) {
      initialize_ghosts();
      copy_board_to_ghost1();
      number= number_of_squares_in_ghost1_column((UCHAR)iterations);
      if(number == 8) {
 move_list[iterations]= 0;
 }
      else {
 ghost1[8 - number - 1][iterations]= opponent;
 move_list[iterations]= search_ghost1();
 }
      }

   ////////////////////////////////
   // return immediately to
   // block loss
```

```
      for(ctr= 0; ctr < 8; ctr++) {
         if((move_list[ctr] == opponent) ) {
            return ctr;
            }
         }

   return NO_IMMEDIATE_LOSS;
}
```

8.10 Can Dr. Plopper set up a forced win in two moves?

This powerful function seeks to find lethal combinations for Dr. Plopper. When successful, it returns a move which forces the human to set up a win for the Dr. Plopper. Listing 8.10 presents the source code for the create_setup2(...) function.

❑ **Listing 8.10** Source code for the create_setup2(...) function.

```
//////////////////////////////////////
//
// Create setup win in two for Plopper.
//

UCHAR create_setup2(UCHAR turn)
{
UCHAR number, move, opponent;
UCHAR squares[8];
UCHAR result, index;
UCHAR buffer[8];
int   ctr;
int   iterations, iterations2, iterations3;

   if(turn == RED) {
      opponent= BLUE;
      }
   else {
      opponent= RED;
      }
```

```
///////////////////////////
// Make 1-ply move.

for(iterations= 0; iterations < 8; iterations++) {
   initialize_ghosts();
   copy_board_to_ghost1();
   number= number_of_squares_in_ghost1_column((UCHAR)iterations);
   if(number < 8) {

      // Place move in column.

      index= 7 - number;
      ghost1[index][iterations]= turn;

      // See if Plopper can win here with second move.

      for(iterations2= 0; iterations2 < 8; iterations2++) {
         copy_ghost1_to_ghost2();
         number=
            number_of_squares_in_ghost2_column((UCHAR)iterations2);

         if(number < 8) {
            number= 7 - number;
            ghost2[number][iterations2]= turn;

            // Check to see if win.

            result= search_ghost2();

            // If win, then assume block by human.

            if(result == turn) {
               ghost2[number][iterations2]= opponent;

               // Now see if Plopper can win again.

               for(iterations3= 0; iterations3 < 8; iterations3++) {
                  copy_ghost2_to_ghost3();
                  number=
                     number_of_squares_in_ghost3_column(
                     (UCHAR)iterations3);
                  if(number < 8) {
                     number= 7 - number;
                     ghost3[number][iterations3]= turn;
```

```
                        // Check to see if win followed after block.

                        result= search_ghost3();
                        if((result == turn) && (coffin[iterations] != 1)) {
                           return iterations;
                        }
                     }
                  }
               }
            }
         }
      }
   return NO_SETUP_FOUND;
}
```

8.11 Dr. Plopper stops a two-move win setup for the human

This powerful function seeks to find if the human has the possibility to set up a forced win combination. If found, this function quickly returns a move to block the human from successfully setting up the lethal combination. Listing 8.11 presents the source code for the `stop_setup2(...)` function.

❏ **Listing 8.11** Source code for the `stop_setup2(...)` function.

```
/////////////////////////////////////////
//
// Stop setup in two moves for human.
//

UCHAR stop_setup2(UCHAR turn)
{
UCHAR number, move, opponent;
UCHAR squares[8];
UCHAR result, index;
UCHAR buffer[8];
int   ctr;
int   iterations, iterations2, iterations3;
```

```
if(turn == RED) {
   opponent= BLUE;
   }
else {
   opponent= RED;
   }

////////////////////////////
// Make 1-ply move.

for(iterations= 0; iterations < 8; iterations++) {
   initialize_ghosts();
   copy_board_to_ghost1();
   number=
      number_of_squares_in_ghost1_column((UCHAR)iterations);
   if(number < 8) {

      // Place move in column.

      index= 7 - number;
      ghost1[index][iterations]= opponent;

         // See if opponent can win here with second move.

         for(iterations2= 0; iterations2 < 8; iterations2++) {
            copy_ghost1_to_ghost2();

            number=
               number_of_squares_in_ghost2_column(
                  (UCHAR)iterations2);

            if(number < 8) {
               number= 7 - number;
               ghost2[number][iterations2]= opponent;

               // Check to see if win.

               result= search_ghost2();

               // If win, then assume block by Plopper.

               if(result == opponent) {
                  ghost2[number][iterations2]= turn;
```

8.12 Dr. Plopper blocks a two-ply fork by human

```
                        // Now see if opponent can win again.

                        for(iterations3= 0; iterations3 < 8; iterations3++) {
                           copy_ghost2_to_ghost3();
                           number=
                              number_of_squares_in_ghost3_column(
                                 (UCHAR)iterations3);
                           if(number < 8) {
                              number= 7 - number;
                              ghost3[number][iterations3]= opponent;

                              // Check to see if win followed after block.

                              result= search_ghost3();
                              if((result == opponent) &&
                                 (coffin[iterations] != 1) &&
                                 (coffin[iterations] != 2)) {
                                 return iterations;
                              }
                           }
                        }
                     }
                  }
               }
            }
         }
      }
   return NO_SETUP_FOUND;
}
```

8.12 Dr. Plopper blocks a two-ply fork by human

This powerful function looks to block the creation of a lethal two-ply fork by the human. It returns the game-saving move if found. Listing 8.12 presents the source code for the `look_ahead_opp(...)` function.

❑ **Listing 8.12** Source code for the `look_ahead_opp(...)` function.

```
////////////////////////////////////
//
// Look to block 2-ply fork by human.
//
```

```
UCHAR look_ahead_opp(UCHAR turn)
{
UCHAR number, move, opponent;
UCHAR squares[8];
UCHAR result, index;
UCHAR buffer[8];
int   ctr;
int   iterations, iterations2;

   if(turn == RED) {
      opponent= BLUE;
      }
   else {
      opponent= RED;
      }

   ////////////////////////////
   // Make 1-ply move.

   for(iterations= 0; iterations < 8; iterations++) {
      initialize_ghosts();
      copy_board_to_ghost1();
      number=
         number_of_squares_in_ghost1_column((UCHAR)iterations);
      if(number < 8) {

         // Place move in column.

         index= 8 - number - 1;
         ghost1[index][iterations]= turn;

         // Check to see if two potential wins found.

         result= search_ghost1_fork_move(turn);

         // If there are two or more wins, then
         // go to next ply and see if you can
         // reduce the double win to one - hopefully.

         if(result >= 2) {

            for(iterations2= 0; iterations2 < 8; iterations2++) {
               copy_board_to_ghost1();

               ghost1[index][iterations]= turn;
```

```
                number=
                    number_of_squares_in_ghost1_column(
                        (UCHAR)iterations2);

                if(number < 8) {

                    // Check to see if two potential wins found.

                    result= search_ghost1_fork_move(turn);

                    if((result < 2) &&
                        (coffin[iterations2] != 1) &&
                        (coffin[iterations2] != 2)) {

                        return iterations2;
                    }
                }
            }
        }
    }

    return NO_FORK_FOUND;
} ∎
```

8.13 Summary

Ply searching can provide very accurate information which can help Dr. Plopper make powerful moves. On the down side, the deeper your ply searches, the longer they will take. Since we took the OAI paradigm's posture of creating a program which selects moves in a human time frame, we knew that we'd have to avoid deep ply searches.

Once the decision to avoid deep ply searches was firm, we knew that we'd have to find the point where program instinct should stop and program learning should begin. That point will be discussed fully in the first section on program learning, in Chapter 11.

chapter 9

Drop Four program instinct: Primitive pattern-matching

Listings 9.1 through 9.4 present the source code for functions which implement primitive pattern matching. Note that all moves generated by program learning and by more sophisticated program instinct functions prove far more effective than primitive pattern-matching functions, and consequently will be invoked first.

Many of these functions use the following terminology in their comments:

    O|
    OO

If this pattern of human pieces is found, Dr. Plopper will move in the column where the vertical line is placed, if that space is empty. The ensuing pattern would look like this:

    OX
    OO

Although program instinct moves based on such limited data may be considered weak, they nonetheless provide reasoning beyond randomly generated moves, because they seek to form patterns in a non–willy-nilly fashion.

9.1 Program instinct: non-ply positional moves

Listing 9.1 presents the source code for the do_positional_move(...) function. The program instinct moves generated by this function prove weaker than the program instinct moves drawn from ply searches and moves drawn from program learning.

❏ **Listing 9.1** Source code for the do_positional_move(...) function.

```
/////////////////////////////////////
//
// Make positional move.
//

UCHAR do_positional_move( UCHAR turn )
{
UCHAR move= 0;
UCHAR squares[8];
int   iterations;
int   row;

   // Initialize column number array.

   for( iterations= 0; iterations < 8; iterations++ ) {
      move= number_of_squares_in_column( ( UCHAR )iterations );
      squares[iterations]= move;
   }

   // If four squares high, then add diag search.

   if( ( squares[3] >= 3 ) && ( squares[4] >= 3 ) ) {

      for( row= 5; row >= 0; row-- ) {
         if( board[row][3] == turn ) {
            if( ( squares[2] == 6 - row ) && ( !coffin[2] ) ) {
               return 2;
            }
            if( ( squares[1] == 5 - row ) && ( !coffin[1] ) ) {
               return 1;
            }
            if( ( squares[0] == 4 - row ) && ( !coffin[0] ) ) {
               return 0;
            }
         }
```

```
            if( board[row][4] == turn ) {
               if( ( squares[5] == 6 - row ) && ( !coffin[5] ) ) {
                  return 5;
                  }
               if( ( squares[6] == 5 - row ) && ( !coffin[6] ) ){
                  return 6;
                  }
               if( ( squares[7] == 4 - row )  && ( !coffin[7] ) ){
                  return 7;
                  }
               }
            }
      }

      // Fill two center columns first.

      if( ( squares[3] == 1 ) && ( !squares[4] ) && ( !coffin[4] ) ) {
         return 4;
         }
      else if( ( !squares[3] ) && ( squares[4] == 1 ) && ( !coffin[3] ) ) {
         return 3;
         }
      else if( ( squares[3] < 5 ) && ( !coffin[3] ) ) {
         return 3;
         }
      else if( ( squares[4] < 5 ) && ( !coffin[4] ) ) {
         return 4;
         }
      else {
         return 8;
         }
   } ■
```

9.2 *Program instinct: opening book positional moves*

Listing 9.2 presents the source code for the `opening_book_first(...)` function. This non-ply pattern response function proves better than a randomly generated move function, but not by much.

❑ **Listing 9.2** Source code for the `opening_book_first(...)` function.

```
///////////////////////////////////////
//
// Early opening book positional moves.
//

UCHAR opening_book_first( UCHAR turn )
{
UCHAR move, opponent;
UCHAR squares[8];
int   iterations;
int   row, col;

   // Initialize column number array.

   for( iterations= 0; iterations < 8; iterations++ ) {
      move= number_of_squares_in_column( ( UCHAR )iterations );
      squares[iterations]= move;
      }

   if( turn == RED ) {
      opponent= BLUE;
      }
   else {
      opponent= RED;
      }

   // Danger!
   //
   // O|      |O
   // OO or   OO

   for( row= 7; row > 2; row-- ) {
      for( col= 1; col < 7; col++ ) {
         if( ( board[row][col] == opponent ) &&
             ( board[row][col + 1] == opponent ) &&
             ( board[row - 1][col] == opponent ) &&
             ( !board[row - 1][col + 1] ) &&
             ( !coffin[col + 1] ) ) {
            return col + 1;
            }
```

9.2 PROGRAM INSTINCT: OPENING BOOK POSITIONAL MOVES

```
            if( ( board[row][col] == opponent ) &&
                ( board[row][col + 1] == opponent ) &&
                ( !board[row - 1][col] ) &&
                ( board[row - 1][col + 1] == opponent ) &&
                ( !coffin[col] ) ) {
                return col;
            }
        }
   }
   // Row 7 OO block.
   for( col= 0; col < 6; col++ ) {
        if( ( !board[7][col] ) &&
            ( board[7][col + 1] == opponent ) &&
            ( board[7][col + 2] == opponent ) &&
            ( !coffin[col] ) ) {
            return col;
        }
   }
   // Right side decisions.
   for( row= 5; row > 2; row-- ) {
        for( col= 4; col < 7; col++ ) {
            if( ( !board[row][col] ) &&
                ( board[row + 1][col + 1] == opponent ) &&
                ( board[row + 2][col + 2] == opponent ) &&
                ( board[row + 1][col] ) &&
                ( !coffin[col] ) ) {
                return col;
            }
        }
   }
   // Build structure.
   // OX
   // XO
   // OX
   for( row= 7; row > 4; row-- ) {
        for( col= 1; col < 7; col++ ) {
            if( ( board[row][col] == opponent ) &&
                ( board[row][col + 1] == turn ) &&
                ( !board[row - 1][col] ) &&
                ( !coffin[col] ) ) {
                return col;
            }
```

```
            if( ( board[row][col] == turn ) &&
                ( board[row][col + 1] == opponent ) &&
                ( !board[row - 1][col + 1] ) &&
                ( !coffin[col + 1] ) ) {
              return col + 1;
              }
            //
            //   OX
            //   XO
            //  |OX
            if( ( !board[row][col] ) &&
                ( board[row][col + 1] == opponent ) &&
                ( board[row - 1][col + 1] == turn ) &&
                ( board[row - 2][col + 1] == opponent ) &&
                ( board[row - 2][col + 2] == turn ) &&
                ( !coffin[col] ) ) {
              return col;
              }
            //
            //   XO
            //   OX
            //   XO|
            if( ( board[row][col] == turn ) &&
                ( board[row][col + 1] == opponent ) &&
                ( board[row - 1][col] == opponent ) &&
                ( board[row - 1][col + 1] == turn ) &&
                ( board[row - 2][col + 1] == opponent ) &&
                ( board[row - 2][col] == turn ) &&
                ( !board[row][col + 2] ) &&
                ( col + 2 < 8 ) &&
                ( !coffin[col + 2] ) ) {
              return col + 2;
              }
            }
          }

      return NO_BOOK_MOVE;
    } ∎
```

9.3 Program instinct: opening book defensive moves

Listing 9.3 presents the source code for the `opening_book_defensive(...)` function. This non-ply program instinct function tries, in a primitive way, to prevent the formation of patterns which might prove favorable to the human at some later time during game play.

❏ **Listing 9.3** Source code for the `opening _book_defensive(...)` function.

```
/////////////////////////////////////
//
// Opening book defensive moves.
//

UCHAR opening_book_defense( UCHAR turn )
{
UCHAR move, opponent;
UCHAR squares[8];
int   iterations;
int   row, col;

   // Initialize column number array.

   for( iterations= 0; iterations < 8; iterations++ ) {
      move= number_of_squares_in_column( ( UCHAR )iterations );
      squares[iterations]= move;
   }

   if( turn == RED ) {
      opponent= BLUE;
   }
   else {
      opponent= RED;
   }

   for( row= 7; row > 5; row-- ) {
      for( col= 0; col < 6; col++ ) {
```

```
            //x   x
            //O   O
            if( ( board[row][col] == opponent ) &&
                ( !board[row][col + 1] ) &&
                ( board[row][col + 2] == opponent ) &&
                ( !board[row - 1][col] ) ) {
                coffin[col]= 1;
            }
            if( ( board[row][col] == opponent ) &&
                ( !board[row][col + 1] ) &&
                ( board[row][col + 2] == opponent ) &&
                ( !board[row - 1][col + 2] ) ) {
                coffin[col + 2]= 1;
            }
        }
    }
//   ||O
//   AOA
//   OAA
    for( row= 7; row > 3; row-- ) {
        for( col= 0; col < 5; col++ ) {
            //     |
            //     A
            //     A
            // O   A
            if( ( board[row][col] == turn ) &&
                ( !board[row - 1][col + 1] ) &&
                ( !board[row - 2][col + 2] ) &&
                ( !board[row - 3][col + 3] ) &&
                ( board[row - 2][col + 3] ) &&
                ( !coffin[col + 3] ) ) {
                return col + 3;
            }
            //     |
            //     OA
            //     AA
            // O  AA
            if( ( board[row][col] == opponent ) &&
                ( !board[row - 1][col + 1] ) &&
                ( board[row - 2][col + 2] == opponent ) &&
                ( !board[row - 3][col + 3] ) &&
                ( board[row - 2][col + 3] ) &&
                ( !coffin[col + 3] ) ) {
                return col + 3;
            }
```

9.3 PROGRAM INSTINCT: OPENING BOOK DEFENSIVE MOVES

```
//    O
//     A
//    | A
// OAAA
if( ( board[row][col] == opponent ) &&
    ( !board[row - 1][col + 1] ) &&
    ( !board[row - 2][col + 2] ) &&
    ( board[row - 3][col + 3] == opponent ) &&
    ( board[row][col + 1] ) &&
    ( !board[row - 1][col + 1] ) &&
    ( !coffin[col + 1] ) ) {
    return col + 1;
    }
if( ( board[row][col] == opponent ) &&
    ( board[row - 1][col + 1] == opponent ) &&
    ( board[row - 2][col + 2] == opponent ) &&
    ( board[row - 1][col + 1] ) &&
    ( !board[row - 2][col + 1] ) &&
    ( !coffin[col + 1] ) ) {
    return col + 1;
    }
if( ( board[row][col] == opponent ) &&
    ( board[row - 1][col + 1] == opponent ) &&
    ( board[row - 2][col + 2] == opponent ) &&
    ( board[row - 1][col] ) &&
    ( !board[row - 2][col] ) &&
    ( !coffin[col] ) ) {
    return col;
    }
//
//   O
//  |O
// OA
if( ( board[row][col] == opponent ) &&
    ( board[row - 1][col + 1] == opponent ) &&
    ( board[row - 2][col + 1] == opponent ) &&
    ( !board[row - 1][col] ) &&
    ( !coffin[col] ) ) {
    return col;
    }
}
}
```

```
//   ||O
//   AOA
//   OAA
for( row= 7; row > 3; row-- ) {
   for( col= 3; col < 8; col++ ) {
      //      |
      //      A
      //      A
      //   O  A
      if( ( board[row][col] == turn ) &&
          ( !board[row - 1][col - 1] ) &&
          ( !board[row - 2][col - 2] ) &&
          ( !board[row - 3][col - 3] ) &&
          ( board[row - 2][col - 3] ) &&
          ( !coffin[col - 3] ) ) {
         return col - 3;
         }
      //      |
      //    OA
      //    AA
      // O AA
      if( ( board[row][col] == opponent ) &&
          ( !board[row - 1][col - 1] ) &&
          ( board[row - 2][col - 2] == opponent ) &&
          ( !board[row - 3][col - 3] ) &&
          ( board[row - 2][col - 3] ) &&
          ( !coffin[col - 3] ) ) {
         return col - 3;
         }
      // O
      // A
      // A |
      // AAAO
      if( ( board[row][col] == opponent ) &&
          ( !board[row - 1][col - 1] ) &&
          ( !board[row - 2][col - 2] ) &&
          ( board[row - 3][col - 3] == opponent ) &&
          ( board[row][col - 1] ) &&
          ( !board[row - 1][col - 1] ) &&
          ( !coffin[col - 1] ) ) {
         return col - 1;
         }
```

9.3 PROGRAM INSTINCT: OPENING BOOK DEFENSIVE MOVES

```
            if( ( board[row][col] == opponent ) &&
                ( board[row - 1][col - 1] == opponent ) &&
                ( board[row - 2][col - 2] == opponent ) &&
                ( board[row - 1][col - 1] ) &&
                ( !board[row - 2][col - 1] ) &&
                ( !coffin[col - 1] ) ) {
                return col - 1;
                }
            if( ( board[row][col] == opponent ) &&
                ( board[row - 1][col - 1] == opponent ) &&
                ( board[row - 2][col - 2] == opponent ) &&
                ( board[row - 1][col] ) &&
                ( !board[row - 2][col] ) &&
                ( !coffin[col] ) ) {
                return col;
                }
            //
            //   O
            //   |O
            //   OA
            if( ( board[row][col] == opponent ) &&
                ( board[row - 1][col - 1] == opponent ) &&
                ( board[row - 2][col - 1] == opponent ) &&
                ( !board[row - 1][col] ) &&
                ( !coffin[col] ) ) {
                return col;
                }
            }
        }
    for( col= 0; col < 5; col++ ) {
        for( row= 7; row > 3; row-- ) {
            //
            //    O
            //     A
            //    OAA
            if( ( !board[row][col] ) &&
                ( board[row - 1][col + 1] == opponent ) &&
                ( !board[row - 2][col + 2] ) &&
                ( board[row - 3][col + 3] == opponent ) &&
                ( board[row - 1][col + 2] ) &&
                ( !coffin[col + 2] ) ) {
                return col + 2;
                }
```

```
//
//    O
//    A
//  | A
// OA A
if( ( board[row][col] == opponent ) &&
    ( !board[row - 1][col + 1] ) &&
    ( !board[row - 2][col + 2] ) &&
    ( board[row - 3][col + 3] == opponent ) &&
    ( board[row][col + 1] ) &&
    ( !coffin[col + 1] ) ) {
   return col + 1;
   }
//
//
//    O
//   |A
// OAA
if( ( board[row][col] == opponent ) &&
    ( !board[row - 1][col + 1] ) &&
    ( board[row - 2][col + 2] == opponent ) &&
    ( !board[row - 3][col + 3] ) &&
    ( board[row][col + 1] ) &&
    ( !coffin[col + 1] ) ) {
   return col + 1;
   }
//
//
//   |
//   OA
// OAA
if( ( board[row][col] == opponent ) &&
    ( board[row - 1][col + 1] == opponent ) &&
    ( !board[row - 2][col + 2] ) &&
    ( !board[row - 3][col + 3] ) &&
    ( board[row - 1][col + 2] ) &&
    ( !coffin[col + 2] ) ) {
   return col + 2;
   }
//
//   |
//   A
//  O A
// OA A
```

9.3 PROGRAM INSTINCT: OPENING BOOK DEFENSIVE MOVES

```
            if( ( board[row][col] == opponent ) &&
                ( board[row - 1][col + 1] == opponent ) &&
                ( !board[row - 2][col + 2] ) &&
                ( !board[row - 3][col + 3] ) &&
                ( board[row - 2][col + 3] ) &&
                ( !coffin[col + 3] ) ) {
              return col + 3;
            }
         //
         //      O
         //      |A
         //       AA
         // O AA
            if( ( board[row][col] == opponent ) &&
                ( !board[row - 1][col + 1] ) &&
                ( !board[row - 2][col + 2] ) &&
                ( board[row - 3][col + 3] == opponent ) &&
                ( board[row - 1][col + 2] ) &&
                ( !coffin[col + 2] ) ) {
              return col + 2;
            }
         }
      }

      for( col= 3; col < 6; col++ ) {
         for( row= 7; row > 3; row-- ) {
         //
         //      O
         //      A
         //   OAA
         //    AAA
            if( ( !board[row][col] ) &&
                ( board[row - 1][col - 1] == opponent ) &&
                ( !board[row - 2][col - 2] ) &&
                ( board[row - 3][col - 3] == opponent ) &&
                ( board[row - 1][col - 2] ) &&
                ( !coffin[col - 2] ) ) {
              return col - 2;
            }
         //
         //      O
         //      A
         //    | A
         // OA A
```

```
       if( ( board[row][col] == opponent ) &&
           ( !board[row - 1][col - 1] ) &&
           ( !board[row - 2][col - 2] ) &&
           ( board[row - 3][col - 3] == opponent ) &&
           ( board[row][col - 1] ) &&
           ( !coffin[col - 1] ) ) {
           return col - 1;
           }
       //
       //
       //    O
       //    |A
       // OAA
       if( ( board[row][col] == opponent ) &&
           ( !board[row - 1][col - 1] ) &&
           ( board[row - 2][col - 2] == opponent ) &&
           ( !board[row - 3][col - 3] ) &&
           ( board[row][col - 1] ) &&
           ( !coffin[col - 1] ) ) {
           return col - 1;
           }
       //
       //
       //    |
       //   OA
       // OAA
       if( ( board[row][col] == opponent ) &&
           ( board[row - 1][col - 1] == opponent ) &&
           ( !board[row - 2][col - 2] ) &&
           ( !board[row - 3][col - 3] ) &&
           ( board[row - 1][col - 2] ) &&
           ( !coffin[col - 2] ) ) {
           return col - 2;
           }
       //
       //     |
       //     A
       //   O A
       // OA A
```

9.3 PROGRAM INSTINCT: OPENING BOOK DEFENSIVE MOVES

```
           if( ( board[row][col] == opponent ) &&
               ( board[row - 1][col - 1] == opponent ) &&
               ( !board[row - 2][col - 2] ) &&
               ( !board[row - 3][col - 3] ) &&
               ( board[row - 2][col - 3] ) &&
               ( !coffin[col - 3] ) ) {
               return col - 3;
               }
           //
           //      O
           //     |A
           //     AA
           // O  AA
           if( ( board[row][col] == opponent ) &&
               ( !board[row - 1][col - 1] ) &&
               ( !board[row - 2][col - 2] ) &&
               ( board[row - 3][col - 3] == opponent ) &&
               ( board[row - 1][col - 2] ) &&
               ( !coffin[col - 2] ) ) {
               return col + 2;
               }
        }
     }

     for( col= 0; col < 5; col++ ) {
        for( row= 6; row > 3; row-- ) {
           //
           //
           //   OO |
           //   AA  A
           if( ( board[row][col] == opponent ) &&
               ( board[row][col + 1] == opponent ) &&
               ( !board[row][col + 2] ) &&
               ( !board[row][col + 3] ) &&
               ( board[row + 1][col + 3] ) &&
               ( !coffin[col + 3] ) ) {
               return col + 3;
               }
           //
           //
           //   O O|
           //   A AA
```

```
            if( ( board[row][col] == opponent ) &&
                ( !board[row][col + 1] ) &&
                ( board[row][col + 2]== opponent ) &&
                ( !board[row][col + 3] ) &&
                ( board[row + 1][col + 3] ) &&
                ( !coffin[col + 3] ) ) {
                return col + 3;
                }
         //
         //
         //   |0 0
         //    AA A
            if( ( !board[row][col] ) &&
                ( board[row][col + 1]    == opponent ) &&
                ( !board[row][col + 2] ) &&
                ( board[row][col + 3] == opponent ) &&
                ( board[row + 1][col] ) &&
                ( !coffin[col] ) ) {
                return col;
                }
            }
        }

//
//    |
//   000
//   AAA

   for( row= 7; row > 2; row-- ) {
      for( col= 0; col < 6; col++ ) {
         if( ( board[row][col] == opponent ) &&
             ( board[row][col + 1] == opponent ) &&
             ( board[row][col + 2] == opponent ) &&
             ( !board[row - 1][col + 1] ) &&
             ( !coffin[col + 1] ) ) {
             return col + 1;
             }
         }
      }

//
//    0
//   |0
//   0A
```

9.3 PROGRAM INSTINCT: OPENING BOOK DEFENSIVE MOVES

```
for( row= 7; row > 2; row-- ) {
   for( col= 0; col < 7; col++ ) {
      if( ( board[row][col] == opponent ) &&
          ( board[row - 1][col + 1] == opponent ) &&
          ( board[row - 2][col + 1] == opponent ) &&
          ( !board[row - 1][col] ) &&
          ( !coffin[col] ) ) {
         return col;
      }
   }
}

//
// O
// O|
// AO

for( row= 7; row > 2; row-- ) {
   for( col= 1; col < 8; col++ ) {
      if( ( board[row][col] == opponent ) &&
          ( board[row - 1][col - 1] == opponent ) &&
          ( board[row - 2][col - 1] == opponent ) &&
          ( !board[row - 1][col] ) &&
          ( !coffin[col] ) ) {
         return col;
      }
   }
}

//    |
//   OO
//   O

for( row= 7; row > 2; row-- ) {
   for( col= 0; col < 7; col++ ) {
      if( ( board[row][col] == opponent ) &&
          ( board[row - 1][col] == opponent ) &&
          ( board[row - 1][col + 1] == opponent ) &&
          ( !board[row - 2][col + 1] ) &&
          ( !coffin[col + 1] ) ) {
         return col + 1;
      }
   }
}
```

```
//
// |
// OO
//  O

for( row= 7; row > 2; row-- ) {
   for( col= 1; col < 8; col++ ) {
      if( ( board[row][col] == opponent ) &&
          ( board[row - 1][col] == opponent ) &&
          ( board[row - 1][col - 1] == opponent ) &&
          ( !board[row - 2][col - 1] ) &&
          ( !coffin[col - 1] ) ) {
         return col - 1;
         }
      }
   }

for( row= 7; row > 2; row-- ) {
   for( col= 0; col < 5; col++ ) {
      if( ( board[row][col] == opponent ) &&
          ( board[row - 1][col] == opponent ) &&
          ( board[row - 1][col + 1] == opponent ) &&
          ( !board[row - 2][col + 1] ) &&
          ( !coffin[col + 1] ) ) {
         return col + 1;
         }
      }
   }

for( row= 7; row > 2; row-- ) {
   for( col= 2; col < 8; col++ ) {
      if( ( board[row][col] == opponent ) &&
          ( board[row - 1][col] == opponent ) &&
          ( board[row - 2][col - 1] == opponent ) &&
          ( !board[row - 1][col - 1] ) &&
          ( !coffin[col - 1] ) ) {
         return col - 1;
         }
      }
   }
```

9.3 PROGRAM INSTINCT: OPENING BOOK DEFENSIVE MOVES

```
row= 7;
for( col= 0; col < 5; col++ ) {
   if( ( board[row][col] == opponent ) &&
       ( !board[row][col + 1] ) &&
       ( board[row - 3][col + 3] == opponent ) ) {
      coffin[col + 1]= 1;
      break;
      }
   }

row= 4;
for( col= 0; col < 5; col++ ) {
   if( ( board[row][col] == opponent ) &&
       ( !board[row + 3][col + 2] ) &&
       ( board[row + 3][col + 3] == opponent ) ) {
      coffin[col + 2]= 1;
      break;
      }
   }

for( row= 6; row > 4; row-- ) {
   for( col= 0; col < 6; col++ ) {
      if( ( board[row][col] == opponent ) &&
          ( board[row][col + 1] == opponent ) &&
          ( !board[row][col + 2] ) &&
          ( board[row + 1][col + 2] ) &&
          ( !coffin[col + 2] ) ) {
         return col + 2;
         }
      }
   }

for( row= 6; row > 4; row-- ) {
   for( col= 1; col < 8; col++ ) {
      if( ( board[row][col] == opponent ) &&
          ( board[row][col + 1] == opponent ) &&
          ( !board[row][col - 1] ) &&
          ( board[row + 1][col -1] ) &&
          ( !coffin[col - 1] ) ) {
         return col - 1;
         }
      }
   }
```

```
for( row= 6; row > 4; row-- ) {
   for( col= 0; col < 7; col++ ) {
      if( ( board[row][col] == opponent ) &&
          ( board[row - 1][col - 1] == opponent ) &&
          ( !board[row + 1][col + 1] ) &&
          ( !coffin[col + 1] ) ) {
         return col + 1;
         }
      }
   }

for( row= 6; row > 4; row-- ) {
   for( col= 2; col < 8; col++ ) {
      if( ( board[row][col] == opponent ) &&
          ( board[row - 1][col - 1] == opponent ) &&
          ( !board[row - 2][col - 2] ) &&
          ( !coffin[col - 2] ) ) {
         return col - 2;
         }
      }
   }

row= 5;
for( col= 2; col < 8; col++ ) {
   if( ( board[row][col] == opponent ) &&
       ( board[row - 1][col + 1] == opponent ) &&
       ( !board[row + 2][col - 2] ) &&
       ( !coffin[col - 2] ) ) {
      return col - 2;
      }
   }

for( col= 0; col < 5; col++ ) {
   if( ( board[row][col] == opponent ) &&
       ( board[row - 1][col - 1] == opponent ) &&
       ( !board[row + 2][col + 2] ) &&
       ( !coffin[col + 2] ) ) {
      return col + 2;
      }
   }
```

9.3 PROGRAM INSTINCT: OPENING BOOK DEFENSIVE MOVES

```
for( row= 7; row > 2; row-- ) {
   for( col= 0; col < 5; col++ ) {
      if( ( board[row][col] == opponent ) &&
          ( board[row - 1][col] == opponent ) &&
          ( !board[row - 2][col] ) &&
          ( board[row - 2][col + 1] == opponent ) &&
          ( board[row - 2][col + 2] == opponent ) &&
          ( !coffin[col] ) ) {
         return col;
         }
      }
   }

for( row= 7; row > 2; row-- ) {
   for( col= 2; col < 8; col++ ) {
      if( ( board[row][col] == opponent ) &&
          ( board[row - 1][col] == opponent ) &&
          ( !board[row - 2][col] ) &&
          ( board[row - 2][col - 1] == opponent ) &&
          ( board[row - 2][col - 2] == opponent ) &&
          ( !coffin[col] ) ) {
         return col;
         }
      }
   }

for( row= 7; row > 2; row-- ) {
   for( col= 0; col < 5; col++ ) {
      if( ( board[row][col] == turn ) &&
          ( board[row - 1][col] == turn ) &&
          ( !board[row - 2][col] ) &&
          ( board[row - 2][col + 1] == turn ) &&
          ( board[row - 2][col + 2] == turn ) &&
          ( !coffin[col] ) ) {
         return col;
         }
      }
   }
```

```
for( row= 7; row > 2; row-- ) {
   for( col= 2; col < 8; col++ ) {
      if( ( board[row][col] == turn ) &&
          ( board[row - 1][col] == turn ) &&
          ( !board[row - 2][col] ) &&
          ( board[row - 2][col - 1] == turn ) &&
          ( board[row - 2][col - 2] == turn ) &&
          ( !coffin[col] ) ) {
         return col;
      }
   }
}

for( row= 6; row > 3; row-- ) {
   for( col= 0; col < 5; col++ ) {
      if( ( board[row][col] == opponent ) &&
          ( board[row][col + 1] == opponent ) &&
          ( !board[row][col + 2] ) &&
          ( !board[row][col + 3] ) &&
          ( board[row + 1][col + 3] ) &&
          ( !coffin[col + 3] ) ) {
         return col + 3;
      }
   }
}

for( row= 6; row > 3; row-- ) {
   for( col= 3; col < 8; col++ ) {
      if( ( board[row][col] == opponent ) &&
          ( board[row][col - 1] == opponent ) &&
          ( !board[row][col - 2] ) &&
          ( !board[row][col - 3] ) &&
          ( board[row + 1][col - 3] ) &&
          ( !coffin[col - 3] ) ) {
         return col - 3;
      }
   }
}
```

9.3 PROGRAM INSTINCT: OPENING BOOK DEFENSIVE MOVES

```
for( row= 6; row > 3; row-- ) {
   for( col= 0; col < 5; col++ ) {
      if( ( board[row][col] == turn ) &&
          ( board[row][col + 1] == turn ) &&
          ( !board[row][col + 2] ) &&
          ( !board[row][col + 3] ) &&
          ( board[row + 1][col + 3] ) &&
          ( !coffin[col + 3] ) ) {
         return col + 3;
         }
      }
   }

for( row= 6; row > 3; row-- ) {
   for( col= 3; col < 8; col++ ) {
      if( ( board[row][col] == turn ) &&
          ( board[row][col - 1] == turn ) &&
          ( !board[row][col - 2] ) &&
          ( !board[row][col - 3] ) &&
          ( board[row + 1][col - 3] ) &&
          ( !coffin[col - 3] ) ) {
         return col - 3;
         }
      }
   }

for( row= 7; row >= 0; row-- ) {
   for( col= 1; col < 6; col++ ) {
      if( row == 7 ) {
         if( ( board[row][col] == opponent )    &&
             ( board[row][col + 1] == opponent ) ) {
            if( ( !board[row][col - 1] ) && ( !coffin[col - 1] ) ) {
               return col - 1;
               }
            if( ( !board[row][col + 2] ) && ( !coffin[col + 2] ) ) {
               return col + 2;
               }
            }
         }
```

```
            if( row < 7 ) {
                if( ( board[row][col] == opponent )      &&
                    ( board[row][col + 1] == opponent ) ) {
                    if( ( !board[row][col - 1] ) &&
                        ( board[row - 1][col - 1] ) && ( !coffin[col - 1] ) ) {
                        return col - 1;
                    }
                    if( ( !board[row][col + 2] ) &&
                        ( board[row - 1][col + 2] ) && ( !coffin[col + 2] ) ) {
                        return col + 2;
                    }
                }
            }
        }
    }

    for( row= 7; row >= 2; row-- ) {
        for( col= 0; col < 8; col++ ) {

            if( ( board[row][col] == opponent ) &&
                ( board[row - 1][col] == opponent ) &&
                ( !coffin[col] ) && ( !board[row - 2][col] ) ){
                return col;
            }
            if( ( board[row][col] == opponent ) &&
                ( board[row - 1][col] == opponent ) &&
                ( !board[row][col - 1] ) &&
                ( !coffin[col - 1] ) && ( col > 0 ) ) {
                return col - 1;
            }

            //    |      |     |
            //    H      H     H
            //    H            H  H

            if( ( board[row][col] == opponent ) &&
                ( board[row - 1][col - 1] == opponent ) &&
                ( squares[col - 2] == 2 ) &&
                ( !coffin[col - 2] ) && ( col > 2 ) ) {
                return col - 2;
            }
```

```
            if( ( board[row][col] == opponent ) &&
                ( board[row - 1][col + 1] == opponent ) &&
                ( squares[col + 2] == 2 ) &&
                ( !coffin[col + 2] ) && ( col < 5 ) ) {
              return col + 2;
              }
          }
      }
  for( col= 0; col < 8; col++ ) {
    //
    //    | H
    //    H P
    if ( board[7][col] == turn ) {
      if( ( col < 5 ) &&
          ( squares[col+1] == 1 ) &&
          ( !coffin[col+1] ) && ( col < 7 ) ) {
        return col+1;
        }
      if( ( col > 2 ) &&
          ( squares[col-1] == 1 ) &&
          ( !coffin[col-1] ) && ( col > 0 ) ) {
        return col-1;
        }
      }
    //
    //    | H
    //    x H
    if( ( board[7][col] == opponent ) &&
        ( board[6][col] == opponent ) &&
        ( board[7][col - 1] ) && ( !board[6][col - 1] ) &&
        ( !coffin[col - 1] ) && ( col > 0 ) ) {
      return col - 1;
      }
    }
  for( row= 7; row >= 4; row-- ) {
    for( col= 0; col < 8; col++ ) {
      if( ( board[row][col] == opponent ) &&
          ( board[row - 1][col] == opponent ) &&
          ( !board[row - 2][col] ) && ( !coffin[col] ) ) {
        return col;
        }
```

```
            if ( ( board[row][col] == opponent ) && ( col<4 ) ) {
              if( ( !board[row - 1][col+1] ) && ( !coffin[col+1] ) ) {
                  return col+1;
                  }
              if( ( !board[row][col-1] ) && ( !coffin[col-1] ) && ( col > 0 ) ) {
                  return col-1;
                  }
              }

          if( ( board[row][col] == opponent ) && ( col>3 ) ) {
              if( ( !board[row][col-1] ) && ( !coffin[col-1] ) )  {
                  return col-1;
                  }
              if ( ( !board[row][col+1] ) && ( !coffin[col+1] ) && ( col < 7 ) ) {
                  return col+1;
                  }
               }
            }
         }
     for( row= 6; row >= 4; row-- ) {
        for( col= 0; col < 8; col++ ) {

              if( ( board[row][col] == opponent ) &&
                  ( board[row][col + 1] == opponent ) &&
                  ( !board[row][col - 1] ) &&
                  ( board[row + 1][col - 1] ) &&
                  ( col > 0 ) &&
                  ( !coffin[col - 1] ) ) {
                  return col - 1;
                  }
              if( ( board[row][col] == opponent ) &&
                  ( board[row][col + 1] == opponent ) &&
                  ( !board[row][col + 2] ) &&
                  ( board[row + 1][col + 2] ) &&
                  ( col <= 5 ) &&
                  ( !coffin[col + 2] ) ) {
                  return col + 2;
                  }
            }
        }
    return NO_BOOK_MOVE;

} ■
```

9.4 Program instinct: opening book offensive moves

Listing 9.4 presents the source code for the `opening_book_offensive(...)` function. This primitive program instinct function tries to create opportunities for Dr. Plopper to eventually construct piece patterns which might lead to the formation of three-filled patterns.

❑ **Listing 9.4** Source code for the `opening_book_offensive(...)` function.

```
//////////////////////////////////////
//
// Opening book offensive pattern
// creation moves.
//

UCHAR opening_book_offense( UCHAR turn )
{
UCHAR move;
UCHAR squares[8];
int   iterations;
int   row, col;

   // Initialize column number array.

   for( iterations= 0; iterations < 8; iterations++ ) {
      move= number_of_squares_in_column( ( UCHAR )iterations );
      squares[iterations]= move;
   }

   for( row= 7; row > 3; row-- ) {
      for( col= 1; col < 5; col++ ) {
         //
         // |T T|
         if( ( !board[row][col] ) &&
            ( board[row][col + 1] == turn ) &&
            ( !board[row][col + 2] ) &&
            ( board[row][col + 3] == turn ) &&
            ( board[row - 1][col] ) &&
            ( !coffin[col] ) ) {
            return col;
         }
```

```
            if( ( board[row][col] == turn ) &&
                ( !board[row][col + 1] ) &&
                ( board[row][col + 2] == turn ) &&
                ( !board[row][col + 3] ) &&
                ( board[row - 1][col + 3] ) &&
                ( !coffin[col + 3] ) ) {
                return col + 3;
                }
            }
        }

   for( col= 0; col < 5; col++ ) {
      for( row= 7; row > 3; row-- ) {
         //
         //   O
         //    A
         // OAA
         if( ( !board[row][col] ) &&
             ( board[row - 1][col + 1] == turn ) &&
             ( !board[row - 2][col + 2] ) &&
             ( board[row - 3][col + 3] == turn ) &&
             ( board[row - 1][col + 2] ) &&
             ( !coffin[col + 2] ) ) {
             return col + 2;
             }
         //
         //   O
         //    A
         //   | A
         // OA A
         if( ( board[row][col] == turn ) &&
             ( !board[row - 1][col + 1] ) &&
             ( !board[row - 2][col + 2] ) &&
             ( board[row - 3][col + 3] == turn ) &&
             ( board[row][col + 1] ) &&
             ( !coffin[col + 1] ) ) {
             return col + 1;
             }
         //
         //
         //   O
         //   |A
         // OAA
```

9.4 PROGRAM INSTINCT: OPENING BOOK OFFENSIVE MOVES

```
    if( ( board[row][col] == turn ) &&
        ( !board[row - 1][col + 1] ) &&
        ( board[row - 2][col + 2] == turn ) &&
        ( !board[row - 3][col + 3] ) &&
        ( board[row][col + 1] ) &&
        ( !coffin[col + 1] ) ) {
      return col + 1;
      }
//
//
//    |
//   OA
//  OAA
    if( ( board[row][col] == turn ) &&
        ( board[row - 1][col + 1] == turn ) &&
        ( !board[row - 2][col + 2] ) &&
        ( !board[row - 3][col + 3] ) &&
        ( board[row - 1][col + 2] ) &&
        ( !coffin[col + 2] ) ) {
      return col + 2;
      }
//
//    |
//    A
//   O A
//  OA A
    if( ( board[row][col] == turn ) &&
        ( board[row - 1][col + 1] == turn ) &&
        ( !board[row - 2][col + 2] ) &&
        ( !board[row - 3][col + 3] ) &&
        ( board[row - 2][col + 3] ) &&
        ( !coffin[col + 3] ) ) {
      return col + 3;
      }
//
//     O
//    |A
//    AA
//   O AA
```

```
            if( ( board[row][col] == turn ) &&
                ( !board[row - 1][col + 1] ) &&
                ( !board[row - 2][col + 2] ) &&
                ( board[row - 3][col + 3] == turn ) &&
                ( board[row - 1][col + 2] ) &&
                ( !coffin[col + 2] ) ) {
                return col + 2;
            }
        }
    }

    for( col= 3; col < 8; col++ ) {
        for( row= 7; row > 3; row-- ) {
            //
            //    O
            //    A
            //   OAA
            //   AAA
            if( ( !board[row][col] ) &&
                ( board[row - 1][col - 1] == turn ) &&
                ( !board[row - 2][col - 2] ) &&
                ( board[row - 3][col - 3] == turn ) &&
                ( board[row - 1][col - 2] ) &&
                ( !coffin[col - 2] ) ) {
                return col - 2;
            }
            //
            //    O
            //    A
            //   | A
            // OA A
            if( ( board[row][col] == turn ) &&
                ( !board[row - 1][col - 1] ) &&
                ( !board[row - 2][col - 2] ) &&
                ( board[row - 3][col - 3] == turn ) &&
                ( board[row][col - 1] ) &&
                ( !coffin[col - 1] ) ) {
                return col - 1;
            }
            //
            //
            //    O
            //   |A
            //   OAA
```

9.4 PROGRAM INSTINCT: OPENING BOOK OFFENSIVE MOVES

```
       if( ( board[row][col] == turn ) &&
           ( !board[row - 1][col - 1] ) &&
           ( board[row - 2][col - 2] == turn ) &&
           ( !board[row - 3][col - 3] ) &&
           ( board[row][col - 1] ) &&
           ( !coffin[col - 1] ) ) {
           return col - 1;
           }
//
//
//    |
//   OA
// OAA
       if( ( board[row][col] == turn ) &&
           ( board[row - 1][col - 1] == turn ) &&
           ( !board[row - 2][col - 2] ) &&
           ( !board[row - 3][col - 3] ) &&
           ( board[row - 1][col - 2] ) &&
           ( !coffin[col - 2] ) ) {
           return col - 2;
           }
//
//      |
//     A
//    O A
// OA A
       if( ( board[row][col] == turn ) &&
           ( board[row - 1][col - 1] == turn ) &&
           ( !board[row - 2][col - 2] ) &&
           ( !board[row - 3][col - 3] ) &&
           ( board[row - 2][col - 3] ) &&
           ( !coffin[col - 3] ) ) {
           return col - 3;
           }
//
//      O
//     |A
//     AA
//   O AA
```

```
            if( ( board[row][col] == turn ) &&
                ( !board[row - 1][col - 1] ) &&
                ( !board[row - 2][col - 2] ) &&
                ( board[row - 3][col - 3] == turn ) &&
                ( board[row - 1][col - 2] ) &&
                ( !coffin[col - 2] ) ) {
                return col + 2;
                }
            }
        }

     for( col= 0; col < 5; col++ ) {
        for( row= 6; row > 3; row-- ) {
            //
            //
            //   OO |
            //   AA A
            if( ( board[row][col] == turn ) &&
                ( board[row][col + 1] == turn ) &&
                ( !board[row][col + 2] ) &&
                ( !board[row][col + 3] ) &&
                ( board[row + 1][col + 3] ) &&
                ( !coffin[col + 3] ) ) {
                return col + 3;
                }
            //
            //
            //   0 0|
            //   A AA
            if( ( board[row][col] == turn ) &&
                ( !board[row][col + 1] ) &&
                ( board[row][col + 2]== turn ) &&
                ( !board[row][col + 3] ) &&
                ( board[row + 1][col + 3] ) &&
                ( !coffin[col + 3] ) ) {
                return col + 3;
                }
            //
            //
            //   |0 0
            //   AA A
```

9.4 PROGRAM INSTINCT: OPENING BOOK OFFENSIVE MOVES

```
         if( ( !board[row][col] ) &&
             ( board[row][col + 1]   == turn ) &&
             ( !board[row][col + 2] ) &&
             ( board[row][col + 3] == turn ) &&
             ( board[row + 1][col] ) &&
             ( !coffin[col] ) ) {
           return col;
         }
      }
   }

//
//    O
//   |O
//   OA

for( row= 7; row > 2; row-- ) {
   for( col= 0; col < 7; col++ ) {
      if( ( board[row][col] == turn ) &&
          ( board[row - 1][col + 1] == turn ) &&
          ( board[row - 2][col + 1] == turn ) &&
          ( !board[row - 1][col] ) &&
          ( !coffin[col] ) ) {
         return col;
      }
   }
}

//
// O
// O|
// AO

for( row= 7; row > 2; row-- ) {
   for( col= 1; col < 8; col++ ) {
      if( ( board[row][col] == turn ) &&
          ( board[row - 1][col - 1] == turn ) &&
          ( board[row - 2][col - 1] == turn ) &&
          ( !board[row - 1][col] ) &&
          ( !coffin[col] ) ) {
         return col;
         }
      }
   }
```

```
//    |
//   00
//   0

for( row= 7; row > 2; row-- ) {
   for( col= 0; col < 7; col++ ) {
      if( ( board[row][col] == turn ) &&
         ( board[row - 1][col] == turn ) &&
         ( board[row - 1][col + 1] == turn ) &&
         ( !board[row - 2][col + 1] ) &&
         ( !coffin[col + 1] ) ) {
         return col + 1;
      }
   }
}

//
//  |
//  00
//   0

for( row= 7; row > 2; row-- ) {
   for( col= 1; col < 8; col++ ) {
      if( ( board[row][col] == turn ) &&
         ( board[row - 1][col] == turn ) &&
         ( board[row - 1][col - 1] == turn ) &&
         ( !board[row - 2][col - 1] ) &&
         ( !coffin[col - 1] ) ) {
         return col - 1;
      }
   }
}

for( row= 7; row > 2; row-- ) {
   for( col= 0; col < 5; col++ ) {
      if( ( board[row][col] == turn ) &&
         ( board[row - 1][col] == turn ) &&
         ( board[row - 1][col + 1] == turn ) &&
         ( !board[row - 2][col + 1] ) &&
         ( !coffin[col + 1] ) ) {
         return col + 1;
      }
   }
}
```

```
    for( row= 7; row > 2; row-- ) {
       for( col= 2; col < 8; col++ ) {
          if( ( board[row][col] == turn ) &&
              ( board[row - 1][col] == turn ) &&
              ( board[row - 2][col - 1] == turn ) &&
              ( !board[row - 1][col - 1] ) &&
              ( !coffin[col - 1] ) ) {
             return col - 1;
             }
          }
       }

    return NO_BOOK_MOVE;

} ∎
```

9.5 Summary

This chapter presented primitive pattern-matching functions which generate moves slightly more effective than those generated in a willy-nilly fashion. Moves generated by program learning and more sophisticated program instinct functions must not have generated moves, for one of the weaker pattern-matching functions to be invoked.

chapter 10

Drop Four program instinct: Advanced positional move generation

This chapter introduces the parts of program instinct which generate positional moves based on sophisticated considerations. Certain functions seek to create predefined primitive piece formations on the game board. These primitive piece formations increase the probability of creating three-filled patterns (Chapter 3). The greater the number of three-filled patterns on the board, the greater the probability that a forced win situation will occur. These functions also use ply search techniques. As was mentioned earlier, ply searching produces very accurate and powerful information but can be very time consuming if too many levels are considered. Creating three-filled patterns consumes less time but does not provide information sufficient to generate effective moves.

10.1 In search of a general board position evaluation algorithm

In the early stages of game play, ply searching often proves quite useless. There are just too many possibilities to consider. As the game progresses and potential moves can be eliminated, ply searching becomes a very viable tool. A general position evaluation routine makes great sense in the early stages. The idea is that the greater the number of three-filled patterns there are on the board, the greater one's chances are for winning the game. In addition there are piece formations which might be viewed as precursors to three-filled patterns. Although these formations are not as valuable as three-filled patterns, we believe them important enough to use in the general move evaluation routine.

10.2 Searching for three-filled patterns on the board

The OAI paradigm says that the program should move in a humanlike time frame. Since ply searches would be too time consuming to accomplish this, it seemed sensible to create some other way to generate moves quickly. One possibility was to create three-filled patterns. Listing 10.1 presents the source code for the pattern_search_board(...) function. This returns a move intended to create desirable game board piece patterns for Dr. Plopper and to disrupt desirable game board piece positions for the human.

❑ **Listing 10.1** Source code for the pattern_search_board(...) function.

```
////////////////////////////////////////
//
// Search the board for patterns.
//
CHAR pattern_search_board( UCHAR turn )
{
int    row, col, number;
UCHAR total=0;

   create_win_board();

   for ( col= 0; col < 8; col++ ){
      number= number_of_squares_in_column( col );
      for ( row= 0; row < ( 7-number ); row++ ){
         if ( ( win_board[row][col]==turn ) ||
             ( win_board[row][col]==RED_AND_BLUE ) ) {
            total += 1;
            }
         }
      }

   return total;
} ■
```

10.3 Searching for three-filled patterns on `ghost1`

Listing 10.2 presents the sample source code for the `pattern_search_board(...)` function. This function seeks to find three-filled patterns in the `ghost1` array.

❑ **Listing 10.2** Source code for the `pattern_search_board(...)` function.

```
//////////////////////////////////////////
//
// Search ghost1 for patterns.
//
UCHAR pattern_search_ghost1( UCHAR turn )
{
int   row, col, number;
UCHAR total=0;

   create_win_ghost1();

   for ( col= 0; col < 8; col++ ){
      number= number_of_squares_in_ghost1_column( col );
      for ( row= 0; row < ( 7-number ); row++ ){
         if ( ( win_ghost1[row][col]==turn ) ||
              ( win_ghost1[row][col]==RED_AND_BLUE ) ) {
            total += 1;
            }
         }
      }

   return total;
} ∎
```

10.4 Returning a move which creates three-filled patterns

Listing 10.3 presents the source code for the `check_for_pattern(...)` function. This function returns the move which will create the most three-filled patterns on the game board.

❑ **Listing 10.3** Source code for the check_for_pattern(...) function.

```
///////////////////////////////////////
//
// Check for patterns.
//
UCHAR check_for_pattern( UCHAR turn )
{
UCHAR number;
UCHAR squares[8];
UCHAR win1[8][8];
SHORT moves[9];
UCHAR priority[8];
int   ctr;
int   iterations;
UCHAR opponent;
UCHAR move, result;
UCHAR best_move;
UCHAR row, col, total;
UCHAR first_ply[8];
   if( turn == RED ) {
      opponent= BLUE;
      }
   else {
      opponent= RED;
      }

   // Initialize move list with loss.

   result= pattern_search_board( turn );

   for( iterations= 0; iterations < 8; iterations++ ) {
      total= 0;
      initialize_ghosts();
      copy_board_to_ghost1();
      number=
         number_of_squares_in_ghost1_column( ( UCHAR )iterations );
      if( number == 8 ) {
        moves[iterations]= 0;
         }
      else {
        ghost1[8 - number - 1][iterations]= turn;
        moves[iterations]= pattern_search_ghost1( turn ) - result;
         }
      }
```

```
      best_move= 8;
      moves[best_move] = 0;

      for( ctr= 0; ctr < 8; ctr++ ) {
         if ( moves[ctr] > moves[best_move] ) {
            best_move = ctr;
         }
      }

      if( ( best_move < 8 ) &&
         ( best_move >= 0 ) ) {
         for( ctr= 0; ctr < 8; ctr++ ) {
            if ( ( moves[ctr]==moves[best_move] ) && ( !coffin[ctr] ) ) {
               first_ply[ctr]= 1;
            }
            else {
               first_ply[ctr]= 0;
            }
         }
         move= first_ply_move( turn, first_ply );
         if( move != NO_FIRST_PLY_MOVE ) {
            return move;
         }
         else {
            return NO_PATTERN_DETECTED;
         }
      }
      else {
         return NO_PATTERN_DETECTED;
      }
   }
}  ∎
```

10.5 General position evaluation

Listing 10.4 presents the source code to the `first_ply_move(...)` function. This function works in concert with the `evaluate_board(...)` function (Listing 10.5). This very powerful general position evaluation function-combination often returns moves which are eerily humanlike. They are generated quickly, and often during function testing we'd need to think for a moment to determine why `first_ply_move(...)` returned the move that it did. Overall, this combination might be thought of as being the crown jewel of program instinct.

The evaluate_board(...) function provides a general positional evaluation. Each of the eight possible moves is considered and weighted according to 8 raw scores. Each score evaluates a different positional consideration. These include primitive offensive and defensive game piece patterns. Each of these patterns, located by the primitive positional functions, is weighted according to the values contained in the elements of the weights[8] array. The weighted raw_score for each potential move is summed up in the evaluation_first_ply[8] array.

The evaluate_board(...) function places the raw scores for each move into the evaluation_first_ply[8] array. first_ply_move(...) simply finds the highest score of the evaluation_first_ply[8] array that has not been *coffined* out. This whole system solves the problem of the weak pattern-matching scheme presented in Chapter 9 because it uses all positional considerations at the same time.

Listing 10.5 presents the source code for the evaluate_board(...) function and related data arrays.

❏ **Listing 10.4** Source code for the first_ply_move(...) function.

```
/////////////////////////////////////////////////////////////////
// UCHAR first_ply_move(UCHAR turn, UCHAR flags[8]) chooses the best move
// from the evaluation_first_ply that is allowed the flags array
//

UCHAR first_ply_move(UCHAR turn, UCHAR flags[8])
{
UCHAR lcv, counter, best_move;
UCHAR flag= 1;
UCHAR sequence[8]= { 3, 4, 2, 5, 1, 6, 0, 7 };

// IMPORTANT NOTE:
//   The evaluate_board(turn) function is called
//   before this function is called.
    // The first avaliable move is taken to be the best, and
    // then any better move will replace it and be returned.

    for(lcv= 0; lcv < 8; lcv++) {
       counter= sequence[lcv];
       if ((flag) &&
          (flags[counter]) &&
          (squares[counter]<8) &&
          (!coffin[counter])) {
         flag= 0;
         best_move= counter;
         }
```

10.5 GENERAL POSITION EVALUATION

```
        if ((!flag) &&
            (flags[counter]) &&
            (squares[counter]<8) &&
            (!coffin[counter]) &&
            (evaluation_first_ply[counter] >
             evaluation_first_ply[best_move])) {
          best_move= counter;
          }
        }

    if (!flag) {
      return best_move;
      }
    else {
      return NO_FIRST_PLY_MOVE;
      }
} ■
```

❏ **Listing 10.5** Source code for the `evaluate_board(...)` function and related data arrays.

```
/////////////////////////////////
//   raw_score has eight parts:
//
//   1: double_pat - offense
//   2: double_pat - defense
//   3: pattern    - offense
//   4: pattern    - defense
//   5: open_first - offense
//   6: open_first - defense
//   7: open_offense
//   8: open_defense
//

UCHAR raw_score[8][8]={
                        { 0, 0, 0, 0, 0, 0, 0, 0 },
                        { 0, 0, 0, 0, 0, 0, 0, 0 },
                        { 0, 0, 0, 0, 0, 0, 0, 0 },
                        { 0, 0, 0, 0, 0, 0, 0, 0 },
                        { 0, 0, 0, 0, 0, 0, 0, 0 },
                        { 0, 0, 0, 0, 0, 0, 0, 0 },
                        { 0, 0, 0, 0, 0, 0, 0, 0 },
                        { 0, 0, 0, 0, 0, 0, 0, 0 }};
```

```
SHORT def_weights[8]= { 25, -25, 5, -5, 1, 2, 1, 2 };
SHORT off_weights[8]= { 25, -25, 5, -5, 2, 1, 2, 1 };
SHORT evaluation_first_ply[8]= { 0, 0, 0, 0, 0, 0, 0, 0 };
static UCHAR squares[8];

////////////////////////////////////////////////////////////
// void evaluate_board( UCHAR turn, UCHAR order ) uses
// different types of positional evaluations, and puts
// information in the raw_score array if there is a reason
// to make a certain move.  The information in the
// raw_score array is then multipied by a factor contained
// in a weights array ( offensive or defensive ) and the
// result is placed in the evaluation_first_ply array.
//

void evaluate_board( UCHAR turn, UCHAR order )
{
UCHAR move, opponent, number;
int   iterations, lcv1, lcv2, number1, number2;
int   row, col;
int   total_squares= 0;

   // Initialize arrays and opponent variable.

   for( iterations= 0; iterations < 8; iterations++ ) {
      for( col= 0; col < 8; col++ ) {
         raw_score[iterations][col]= 0;
         }
      evaluation_first_ply[iterations]= 0;
      squares[iterations]=
             number_of_squares_in_column( ( UCHAR )iterations );
      total_squares+= squares[iterations];
      }

   if( turn == RED ) {
      opponent= BLUE;
      }
   else {
      opponent= RED;
      }
```

10.5 GENERAL POSITION EVALUATION

```
// raw_score parts 1-4.
// After a piece is placed in each column,
// the number of single and double threats
// is counted.

for( iterations= 0; iterations < 8; iterations++ ) {
   initialize_ghosts( );
   copy_board_to_ghost1( );
   number= number_of_squares_in_ghost1_column( iterations );
   if( number == 8 ) {
      raw_score[iterations][0]= 0;
      raw_score[iterations][1]= 0;
      raw_score[iterations][2]= 0;
      raw_score[iterations][3]= 0;
      }
    else if ( number == 7 ){
      ghost1[7 - number][iterations]= turn;
      raw_score[iterations][0]=
              count_double_ghost1( turn );
      raw_score[iterations][1]=
              count_double_ghost1( opponent );
      raw_score[iterations][2]=
              pattern_search_ghost1( turn );
      raw_score[iterations][3]=
              pattern_search_ghost1( opponent );
      }
    else {
      ghost1[7 - number][iterations]= turn;
      raw_score[iterations][0]=
              count_double_ghost1( turn );
      raw_score[iterations][2]=
              pattern_search_ghost1( turn );
      if ( coffin[iterations]!= 1 ) {
        ghost1[6 - number][iterations]= opponent;
         }
      raw_score[iterations][1]=
              count_double_ghost1( opponent );
      raw_score[iterations][3]=
              pattern_search_ghost1( opponent );
      }
    }
```

```
// raw_score parts 5-8 consist of various pattern recognition schemes.
// Parts 5 & 7 are offensive, and parts 6 & 8 are defensive. Each
// pattern is "diagramed" before the source code implementation.
// O = "turn" piece, X = "opponent" piece
// A = any piece, | = open space.

// Part 5.

// O|      |O
// OO  or  OO

for( row= 7; row > 2; row-- ) {
   for( col= 1; col < 7; col++ ) {
      if( ( board[row][col] == turn ) &&
          ( board[row][col + 1] == turn ) &&
          ( board[row - 1][col] == turn ) &&
          ( !board[row - 1][col + 1] ) &&
          ( !coffin[col + 1] ) ) {
         raw_score[col + 1][4] += 1;
         }
      if( ( board[row][col] == turn ) &&
          ( board[row][col + 1] == turn ) &&
          ( !board[row - 1][col] ) &&
          ( board[row - 1][col + 1] == turn ) &&
          ( !coffin[col] ) ) {
         raw_score[col][4] += 1;
         }
      }
   }

// | O
//  O O

for( row= 7; row > 1; row-- ) {
  for( col= 2; col < 8; col++ ) {
     if( ( board[row][col] == turn ) &&
         ( board[row][col - 1] == turn ) &&
         ( board[row - 1][col - 1] == turn ) &&
         ( board[row][col - 2] ) &&
         ( !board[row - 1][col - 2] ) &&
         ( !coffin[col - 2] ) ) {
        raw_score[col - 2][4] += 1;
        }
     }
  }
```

10.5 GENERAL POSITION EVALUATION

```
// O |
//   O O

for( row= 7; row > 1; row-- ) {
  for( col= 2; col < 8; col++ ) {
      if( ( board[row][col] == turn ) &&
          ( board[row][col - 1] == turn ) &&
          ( !board[row - 1][col - 1] ) &&
          ( board[row - 1][col - 2] == turn ) &&
          ( !coffin[col - 1] ) ) {
          raw_score[col - 1][4] += 1;
          }
      }
  }

// O O
//   O |

for( row= 7; row > 1; row-- ) {
  for( col= 2; col < 8; col++ ) {
      if( ( !board[row][col] ) &&
          ( board[row][col - 1] == turn ) &&
          ( board[row - 1][col - 1] == turn ) &&
          ( board[row + 1][col] ) &&
          ( board[row - 1][col - 2] == turn ) &&
          ( !coffin[col] ) ) {
          raw_score[col][4] += 1;
          }
      }
  }

//   O |
// O O

for( row= 7; row > 1; row-- ) {
  for( col= 0; col < 6; col++ ) {
      if( ( board[row][col] == turn ) &&
          ( board[row][col + 1] == turn ) &&
          ( board[row - 1][col + 1] == turn ) &&
          ( board[row][col + 2] ) &&
          ( !board[row - 1][col + 2] ) &&
          ( !coffin[col + 2] ) ) {
          raw_score[col + 2][4] += 1;
          }
      }
  }
```

```
//     | 0
// 0 0
for( row= 7; row > 1; row-- ) {
  for( col= 0; col < 6; col++ ) {
      if( ( board[row][col] == turn ) &&
         ( board[row][col + 1] == turn ) &&
         ( board[row - 1][col + 2] == turn ) &&
         ( !board[row - 1][col + 1] ) &&
         ( !coffin[col + 1] ) ) {
         raw_score[col + 1][4] += 1;
         }
      }
   }

//     0 0
// | 0
for( row= 7; row > 1; row-- ) {
  for( col= 0; col < 6; col++ ) {
      if( ( !board[row][col] ) &&
         ( board[row][col + 1] == turn ) &&
         ( board[row - 1][col + 1] == turn ) &&
         ( board[row + 1][col] ) &&
         ( board[row - 1][col + 2] == turn ) &&
         ( !coffin[col] ) ) {
         raw_score[col][4] += 1;
         }
      }
   }

//
//    0
//   |0
//    0
for( row= 7; row > 2; row-- ) {
   for( col= 0; col < 7; col++ ) {
       if( ( board[row][col] == turn ) &&
          ( board[row - 1][col + 1] == turn ) &&
          ( board[row - 2][col + 1] == turn ) &&
          ( !board[row - 1][col] ) &&
          ( !coffin[col] ) ) {
          raw_score[col][4] += 1;
          }
       }
    }
```

10.5 GENERAL POSITION EVALUATION

```
//
// O
// O|
//  O

for( row= 7; row > 2; row-- ) {
   for( col= 1; col < 8; col++ ) {
      if( ( board[row][col] == turn ) &&
          ( board[row - 1][col - 1] == turn ) &&
          ( board[row - 2][col - 1] == turn ) &&
          ( !board[row - 1][col] ) &&
          ( !coffin[col] ) ) {
         raw_score[col][4] += 1;
         }
      }
   }

//    |
//   OO
//   O

for( row= 7; row > 2; row-- ) {
   for( col= 0; col < 7; col++ ) {
      if( ( board[row][col] == turn ) &&
          ( board[row - 1][col] == turn ) &&
          ( board[row - 1][col + 1] == turn ) &&
          ( !board[row - 2][col + 1] ) &&
          ( !coffin[col + 1] ) ) {
         raw_score[col + 1][4] += 1;
         }
      }
   }

//
// |
// OO
//  O

for( row= 7; row > 2; row-- ) {
   for( col= 1; col < 8; col++ ) {
```

```
            if( ( board[row][col] == turn ) &&
                ( board[row - 1][col] == turn ) &&
                ( board[row - 1][col - 1] == turn ) &&
                ( !board[row - 2][col - 1] ) &&
                ( !coffin[col - 1] ) ) {
                raw_score[col - 1][4] += 1;
            }
        }
    }

//    |
//   OOO

    for( row= 7; row > 2; row-- ) {
        for( col= 0; col < 6; col++ ) {
            if( ( board[row][col] == turn ) &&
                ( board[row][col + 1] == turn ) &&
                ( board[row][col + 2] == turn ) &&
                ( !board[row - 1][col + 1] ) &&
                ( !coffin[col + 1] ) ) {
                raw_score[col + 1][4] += 1;
            }
        }
    }

// Part 6

//    |
//   XXX

    for( row= 7; row > 2; row-- ) {
        for( col= 0; col < 6; col++ ) {
            if( ( board[row][col] == opponent ) &&
                ( board[row][col + 1] == opponent ) &&
                ( board[row][col + 2] == opponent ) &&
                ( !board[row - 1][col + 1] ) &&
                ( !coffin[col + 1] ) ) {
                raw_score[col + 1][5] += 1;
            }
        }
    }
```

10.5 GENERAL POSITION EVALUATION

```
// X |    or   | X
// X X         X X

for( row= 7; row > 2; row-- ) {
   for( col= 1; col < 7; col++ ) {
      if( ( board[row][col] == opponent ) &&
          ( board[row][col + 1] == opponent ) &&
          ( board[row - 1][col] == opponent ) &&
          ( !board[row  - 1][col + 1] ) &&
          ( !coffin[col + 1] ) ) {
         raw_score[col + 1][5] += 1;
         }
      if( ( board[row][col] == opponent ) &&
          ( board[row][col + 1] == opponent ) &&
          ( !board[row - 1][col] ) &&
          ( board[row - 1][col + 1] == opponent ) &&
          ( !coffin[col] ) ) {
         raw_score[col][5] += 1;
         }
      }
   }

//
//    X
//   |X
//    X

for( row= 7; row > 2; row-- ) {
   for( col= 0; col < 7; col++ ) {
      if( ( board[row][col] == opponent ) &&
          ( board[row - 1][col + 1] == opponent ) &&
          ( board[row - 2][col + 1] == opponent ) &&
          ( !board[row - 1][col] ) &&
          ( !coffin[col] ) ) {
         raw_score[col][5] += 1;
         }
      }
   }
```

```
//
//  X
//  X|
//   X

for( row= 7; row > 2; row-- ) {
   for( col= 1; col < 8; col++ ) {
      if( ( board[row][col] == opponent ) &&
          ( board[row - 1][col - 1] == opponent ) &&
          ( board[row - 2][col - 1] == opponent ) &&
          ( !board[row - 1][col] ) &&
          ( !coffin[col] ) ) {
         raw_score[col][5] += 1;
         }
      }
   }

//    |
//   XX
//   X

for( row= 7; row > 2; row-- ) {
   for( col= 0; col < 7; col++ ) {
      if( ( board[row][col] == opponent ) &&
          ( board[row - 1][col] == opponent ) &&
          ( board[row - 1][col + 1] == opponent ) &&
          ( !board[row - 2][col + 1] ) &&
          ( !coffin[col + 1] ) ) {
         raw_score[col + 1][5] += 1;
         }
      }
   }

//
//  |
//  XX
//   X

for( row= 7; row > 2; row-- ) {
   for( col= 1; col < 8; col++ ) {
```

10.5 GENERAL POSITION EVALUATION

```
         if( ( board[row][col] == opponent ) &&
             ( board[row - 1][col] == opponent ) &&
             ( board[row - 1][col - 1] == opponent ) &&
             ( !board[row - 2][col - 1] ) &&
             ( !coffin[col - 1] ) ) {
           raw_score[col - 1][5] += 1;
           }
       }
    }

//  | X
//    X X

  for( row= 7; row > 1; row-- ) {
    for( col= 2; col < 8; col++ ) {
        if( ( board[row][col] == opponent ) &&
            ( board[row][col - 1] == opponent ) &&
            ( board[row - 1][col - 1] == opponent ) &&
            ( board[row][col - 2] ) &&
            ( !board[row - 1][col - 2] ) &&
            ( !coffin[col - 2] ) ) {
          raw_score[col - 2][5] += 1;
          }
      }
   }

// X |
//   X X

  for( row= 7; row > 1; row-- ) {
    for( col= 2; col < 8; col++ ) {
        if( ( board[row][col] == opponent ) &&
            ( board[row][col - 1] == opponent ) &&
            ( !board[row - 1][col - 1] ) &&
            ( board[row - 1][col - 2] == opponent ) &&
            ( !coffin[col - 1] ) ) {
          raw_score[col - 1][5] += 1;
          }
       }
     }
```

```
//  X X
//    X |

for( row= 7; row > 1; row-- ) {
   for( col= 2; col < 8; col++ ) {
      if( ( !board[row][col] ) &&
         ( board[row][col - 1] == opponent ) &&
         ( board[row - 1][col - 1] == opponent ) &&
         ( board[row + 1][col] ) &&
         ( board[row - 1][col - 2] == opponent ) &&
         ( !coffin[col] ) ) {
         raw_score[col][5] += 1;
         }
      }
   }

//    X |
//  X X

for( row= 7; row > 1; row-- ) {
   for( col= 0; col < 6; col++ ) {
      if( ( board[row][col] == opponent ) &&
         ( board[row][col + 1] == opponent ) &&
         ( board[row - 1][col + 1] == opponent ) &&
         ( board[row][col + 2] ) &&
         ( !board[row - 1][col + 2] ) &&
         ( !coffin[col + 2] ) ) {
         raw_score[col + 2][5] += 1;
         }
      }
   }

//      | X
//  X X

for( row= 7; row > 1; row-- ) {
   for( col= 0; col < 6; col++ ) {
      if( ( board[row][col] == opponent ) &&
         ( board[row][col + 1] == opponent ) &&
         ( board[row - 1][col + 2] == opponent ) &&
         ( !board[row - 1][col + 1] ) &&
         ( !coffin[col + 1] ) ) {
         raw_score[col + 1][5] += 1;
         }
      }
   }
```

10.5 GENERAL POSITION EVALUATION

```
    //   X X
    // | X

    for( row= 7; row > 1; row-- ) {
      for( col= 0; col < 6; col++ ) {
        if( ( !board[row][col] ) &&
            ( board[row][col + 1] == opponent ) &&
            ( board[row - 1][col + 1] == opponent ) &&
            ( board[row + 1][col] ) &&
            ( board[row - 1][col + 2] == opponent ) &&
            ( !coffin[col] ) ) {
          raw_score[col][5] += 1;
        }
      }
    }

    // Part 7.

    for( row= 7; row >= 2; row-- ) {
      for( col= 0; col < 8; col++ ) {

        // |
        // O
        // O

        if( ( board[row][col] == turn ) &&
            ( board[row - 1][col] == turn ) &&
            ( !coffin[col] ) && ( !board[row - 2][col] ) ){
          raw_score[col][6] += 1;
        }

        //  O
        // |O

        if( ( board[row][col] == turn ) &&
            ( board[row - 1][col] == turn ) &&
            ( !board[row][col - 1] ) &&
            ( !coffin[col - 1] ) && ( col > 0 ) ) {
          raw_score[col - 1][6] += 1;
        }
```

```
            //  O
            //  O|

            if( ( board[row][col] == turn ) &&
                ( board[row - 1][col] == turn ) &&
                ( !board[row][col + 1] ) &&
                ( !coffin[col + 1] ) && ( col < 7 ) ) {
                raw_score[col + 1][6] += 1;
                }
            }
        }

    for( col= 0; col < 8; col++ ) {

        //   | O
        //   A O

        if( ( board[7][col] == turn ) &&
            ( board[6][col] == turn ) &&
            ( board[7][col - 1] ) && ( !board[6][col - 1] ) &&
            ( !coffin[col - 1] ) && ( col > 0 ) ) {
            raw_score[col - 1][6] += 1;
            }

        //   O |
        //   O A

        if( ( board[7][col] == turn ) &&
            ( board[6][col] == turn ) &&
            ( board[7][col + 1] ) && ( !board[6][col + 1] ) &&
            ( !coffin[col + 1] ) && ( col < 7 ) ) {
            raw_score[col + 1][6] += 1;
            }

        if ( board[7][col] == turn ) {

            //   O |

            if( ( col < 4 ) &&
                ( squares[col+1] == 1 ) &&
                ( !coffin[col+1] ) && ( col < 7 ) ) {
                raw_score[col + 1][6] += 1;
                }
```

10.5 GENERAL POSITION EVALUATION

```
            //   | O

         if( ( col > 3 ) &&
             ( squares[col-1] == 1 ) &&
             ( !coffin[col-1] ) && ( col > 0 ) ) {
             raw_score[col - 1][6] += 1;
             }
           }

        if ( board[6][col] == turn ) {

            //    |
            // O A
            // A A

            if( ( col < 4 ) &&
                ( squares[col+1] == 2 ) &&
                ( !coffin[col+1] ) && ( col < 7 ) ) {
                raw_score[col + 1][6] += 1;
                }

            // |
            // A O
            // A A

            if( ( col > 3 ) &&
                ( squares[col-1] == 2 ) &&
                ( !coffin[col-1] ) && ( col > 0 ) ) {
                raw_score[col - 1][6] += 1;
                }
            }
         }
   for( row= 7; row >= 4; row-- ) {
      for( col= 0; col < 8; col++ ) {

      if ( ( board[row][col] == turn ) && ( col<4 ) ) {

        // O |

        if( ( !board[row][col+1] ) && ( !coffin[col+1] )  ) {
            raw_score[col + 1][6] += 2;
            }
```

CHAPTER 10: PROGRAM INSTINCT: POSITIONAL MOVE GENERATION

```
            // | 0
            if( ( !board[row][col-1] ) && ( !coffin[col-1] ) && ( col > 0 ) ) {
               raw_score[col - 1][6] += 1;
               }
            }
         if( ( board[row][col] == turn ) && ( col>3 ) ) {

            // | 0
            if( ( !board[row][col-1] ) && ( !coffin[col-1] ) ) {
              raw_score[col - 1][6] += 2;
              }

            // 0 |
            if ( ( !board[row][col+1] ) && ( !coffin[col+1] ) && ( col < 7 ) ) {
               raw_score[col + 1][6] += 1;
               }
            }
         }
      }

// This gives positional strength to a move
// that will force the opponent to move
// somewhere.
   for ( lcv1= 0; lcv1 < 8; lcv1++ ) {
      initialize_ghosts( );
      copy_board_to_ghost1( );
      number1= number_of_squares_in_ghost1_column( lcv1 );
      if ( number1 != 8 ) {
         ghost1[lcv1][7 - number1]= turn;
         for ( lcv2= 0; lcv2 < 8; lcv2++ ) {
            copy_ghost1_to_ghost2( );
            number2= number_of_squares_in_ghost2_column( lcv2 );
            if ( number2 != 8 ) {
               ghost2[lcv2][7 - number2]= turn;
               if ( search_ghost2( )==turn ) {
                  raw_score[lcv1][6] += 3;
                  }
               }
            }
         }
      }
```

10.5 GENERAL POSITION EVALUATION

```
      // Part 8.

      for( row= 7; row >= 2; row-- ) {
         for( col= 0; col < 8; col++ ) {

            // |
            // X
            // X

            if( ( board[row][col] == opponent ) &&
                ( board[row - 1][col] == opponent ) &&
                ( !coffin[col] ) && ( !board[row - 2][col] ) ){
               raw_score[col][7] += 1;
            }

            //   X
            //  |X

            if( ( board[row][col] == opponent ) &&
                ( board[row - 1][col] == opponent ) &&
                ( !board[row][col - 1] ) &&
                ( !coffin[col - 1] ) && ( col > 0 ) ) {
               raw_score[col - 1][7] += 1;
            }

            // X
            // X|

            if( ( board[row][col] == opponent ) &&
                ( board[row - 1][col] == opponent ) &&
                ( !board[row][col + 1] ) &&
                ( !coffin[col + 1] ) && ( col < 7 ) ) {
               raw_score[col + 1][7] += 1;
            }
         }
      }

      for( col= 0; col < 8; col++ ) {
```

```
        //  | X
        //    X

        if( ( board[7][col] == opponent ) &&
            ( board[6][col] == opponent ) &&
            ( board[7][col - 1] ) && ( !board[6][col - 1] ) &&
            ( !coffin[col - 1] ) && ( col > 0 ) ) {
          raw_score[col - 1][7] += 1;
          }

        // X |
        // X

        if( ( board[7][col] == opponent ) &&
            ( board[6][col] == opponent ) &&
            ( board[7][col + 1] ) && ( !board[6][col + 1] ) &&
            ( !coffin[col + 1] ) && ( col < 7 ) ) {
          raw_score[col + 1][7] += 1;
          }
      }

   for( row= 7; row >= 4; row-- ) {
     for( col= 0; col < 8; col++ ) {

       // X |

       if ( ( board[row][col] == opponent ) && ( col<4 ) ) {
         if( ( !board[row][col+1] ) && ( !coffin[col+1] ) ) {
           raw_score[col + 1][7] += 2;
           }
         }

       //   | X

       if( ( board[row][col] == opponent ) && ( col>3 ) ) {
         if( ( !board[row][col-1] ) && ( !coffin[col-1] ) ) {
           raw_score[col - 1][7] += 2;
           }
         }
       }
     }
   }
```

10.5 GENERAL POSITION EVALUATION

```
// This gives positional strength to a move
// that will prevent the opponent from
// forcing a move.
for ( lcv1= 0; lcv1 < 8; lcv1++ ) {
   initialize_ghosts( );
   copy_board_to_ghost1( );
   number1= number_of_squares_in_ghost1_column( lcv1 );
   if ( number1 != 8 ) {
      ghost1[lcv1][7 - number1]= opponent;
      for ( lcv2= 0; lcv2 < 8; lcv2++ ) {
         copy_ghost1_to_ghost2( );
         number2= number_of_squares_in_ghost2_column( lcv2 );
         if ( number2 != 8 ) {
           ghost2[lcv2][7 - number2]= opponent;
           if ( search_ghost2( )==opponent ) {
             raw_score[lcv1][7] += 3;
             }
           }
         }
      }
   }

 for( col= 0; col < 8; col++ ) {

    if ( board[7][col] == opponent ) {

      //   |
      //    X
      if( ( col < 4 ) &&
          ( squares[col+1] == 1 ) &&
          ( !coffin[col+1] ) && ( col < 7 ) ) {
          raw_score[col + 1][7] += 1;
          }

      // |
      //  X
      if( ( col > 3 ) &&
          ( squares[col-1] == 1 ) &&
          ( !coffin[col-1] ) && ( col > 0 ) ) {
          raw_score[col - 1][7] += 1;
          }
       }
```

```
        if ( board[6][col] == opponent ) {

          //    |
          // X A
          // A

          if( ( col < 4 ) &&
              ( squares[col+1] == 2 ) &&
              ( !coffin[col+1] ) && ( col < 7 ) ) {
              raw_score[col + 1][7] += 1;
              }

          // |
          // A X
          //   A

          if( ( col > 3 ) &&
              ( squares[col-1] == 2 ) &&
              ( !coffin[col-1] ) && ( col > 0 ) ) {
              raw_score[col - 1][7] += 1;
              }
            }
        }

//  This gives positional strength to
//  a move next to a column coffined out.
//  It is both offensive and defensive.

    for ( col= 0; col < 8; col++ ) {
      if ( col == 0 ) {
        if ( coffin[1] ) {
          raw_score[col][6] += 1;
          raw_score[col][7] += 1;
          }
        }
      else if ( col == 7 ) {
        if ( coffin[6] ) {
          raw_score[col][6] += 1;
          raw_score[col][7] += 1;
          }
        }
```

```
      else {
        if ( coffin[col-1] ) {
          raw_score[col][6] += 1;
          raw_score[col][7] += 1;
        }
        if ( coffin[col+1] ) {
          raw_score[col][6] += 1;
          raw_score[col][7] += 1;
        }
      }
    }
  // The evaluation_first_ply is calculated for each column by
  // multiplying each space in the raw_score array by the
  // corresponding weight and adding it the evaluation array.
  for( row= 0; row < 8; row++ ) {
    for( col= 0; col < 8; col++ ) {
      if ( order==SECOND ) {
        evaluation_first_ply[row] +=
            ( ( raw_score[row][col] )*( def_weights[col] ) );
      }
      else {
        evaluation_first_ply[row] +=
            ( ( raw_score[row][col] )*( off_weights[col] ) );
      }
    }
  }
} ■
```

10.6 Summary

The main thrust of this chapter has been to present a solution to the weakness of the primitive program instinct functions presented in Chapter 9. The two important functions in this chapter were first_ply_move(...) and evaluate_board(...). evaluate_board(...) is called before first_ply_move(...), and evaluates the game board by measuring the number of offensive and defensive patterns on the game board. These measurements are then weighted and placed into an array. The first_ply_move(...) function simply scans the array and selects the highest valued move which has not been mediated by a value being placed in the corresponding element of the coffin[8] array.

chapter 11

Drop Four program learning: Analyzing a loss

Program learning occurs at the advanced level of game play. Once a game has been completed and it is determined that the human has won, the move list record is evaluated using the forced move algorithm. Once the kiss of death move has been found and an alternative move which will thwart the loss is selected, the sequence record is stored in the program subconscious. Note that there are many functions involved in record management, because the records are all differentiated to facilitate fast retrieval during game play (as will be seen in Chapter 12). In addition, a piece pattern analysis takes place surrounding the loss position, and a memory marker of the loss pattern is stored in the program subconscious.

Once the analysis has been completed and its results stored in the program subconscious, the information contained there is made available to the program consciousness during game play. Depending on the specific game condition, the forced move or three-filled pattern disruption algorithm will be used to prevent the previously experienced loss.

11.1 Adding a move to the move list

Listing 11.1 presents the source code for the add_list(...) function. The data for the move list are held in the program subconscious. This function takes the move which has been transferred from the program conscious (input from Dr. Plopper or the human—short-term memory) to the program subconscious (the longer-term memory buffer). The data in the program subconscious are a record of moves for the game. In addition, this function creates a record which is a mirror of the original game record. This new record adds to the robustness of the move information transferred from the program conscious.

❑ **Listing 11.1** Source code for the `add_list(...)` function.

```
///////////////////////////////////////////////////////
//
// void add_move_list() saves the level of the analysis,
// the move to be changed, the new move, and the sequence
// of moves into a record in the array.  It also saves the
// mirrored record at the same time.
//

void add_move_list()
{
UCHAR *begin;
int    ctr;
FILE  *in;

   winmov_limit= WINMOV_SIZE / MOVE_OFFSET;

   if ( winmov_count > ( winmov_limit - 2 ) ) {
     return;
     }

   if ( end_move_flag ) {
     write_end_board();
     return;
     }

   // Increment record counter,
   // add original record.

   begin= ( winmov + ( winmov_count * MOVE_OFFSET ) );

   *begin++= 1;

   *begin++= level;
```

```
      *begin++= move_number;

   *begin++= change;

   for( ctr= 0; ctr < 64; ctr++ ) {
      *begin++= move_list[ctr];
   }

   winmov_count+= 1;

   // Create & add mirrored record.

   for ( ctr= 0; ctr < moves_offset; ctr++ ) {
      move_list2[ctr]= 7 - move_list[ctr];
   }

   begin= ( winmov + ( winmov_count * MOVE_OFFSET ) );

   *begin++= 1;

   *begin++= level;

   *begin++= move_number;

   *begin++= 7 - change;

   for( ctr= 0; ctr < 64; ctr++ ) {
      *begin++= move_list2[ctr];
   }

   winmov_count+= 1;

}
```

11.2 First-move analysis

Listing 11.2 presents the source code to the first_move_analysis(...) function. This function examines the data in program subconscious related to the current move list and prepares the implementation of learning via the forced move algorithm by changing the last unforced move before a loss. The first_move_analysis(...) function

(Listing 11.2) and the `second_move_analysis(...)` function (Listing 11.4) were separated to speed up move retrieval during game play.

❑ **Listing 11.2** Source code for the `first_move_analysis(...)` function.

```
/////////////////////////////////////
//
// void first_move_analysis() does the
// level-one analysis by changing
// the last unforced move
// before a loss.
//

void first_move_analysis()
{
int move;

   end_move_flag= 0;

   level= 1;

   move= moves_offset - 2;

   if( move_type[move] == 9 ) {
     end_move_flag= 1;
     }

   while( ( move_type[move] == 1 ) ||
          ( move_type[move] == 3 ) ||
          ( move_list[move] == move_list[move+1] ) ) {
     move= move - 2;
     if( move_type[move] == 9 ) {
        end_move_flag= 1;
        }
     }

   move_number= move;

   change= move_list[move_number + 1];

   new_seq_flag= 1;

} ■
```

11.3 Level-two analysis `opponent_type_move(...)` support function

Listing 11.3 presents the source code to the `opponent_type_move(...)` function. This function inserts a double threat flag into the program subconscious, which is used in a level-two analysis.

❑ **Listing 11.3** Source code for the `opponent_type_move(...)` function.

```
//////////////////////////////////////////////////////////
//
// void opponent_type_move( UCHAR opponent ) inserts the double
// threat flag into the move-type array that is used for the
// level-two analysis.
//

void opponent_type_move( UCHAR opponent )
{
int lcv, found;

   if ( count_double_board( opponent ) ) {
      move_type[moves_offset-1]= 1;
      second_seq_flag= 1;
      }
   else {
      move_type[moves_offset-1]= 0;
      }

} ■
```

11.4 Second move analysis

Listing 11.4 presents the source code to the `second_move_analysis(...)` function. This function examines the data in the program subconscious related to the current move list. It prepares the implementation of learning via the forced move algorithm by changing the last unforced move before a double threat setup would be created by the human player. By "stealing" the human's previously used setup move, Dr. Plopper hopes to avoid the creation of the dangerous pattern.

❏ **Listing 11.4** Source code for the `second_move_analysis(...)` function.

```
/////////////////////////////////////
//
// void second_move_analysis() does the level-two analysis by
// changing the last unforced move before a double threat is
// set up by the player.
//
void second_move_analysis()
{
int move;

   level= 2;

   move= moves_offset - 1;

   while( ( move_type[move] != 1 ) ||
          ( move_type[move-2] !=0 )  ){
     move= move-2;
     }

   move= move - 1;

   while( ( move_type[move] == 1 ) ||
          ( move_type[move] == 3 ) ||
          ( move_list[move] == move_list[move+1] ) ) {
     move= move - 2;
     }

   move_number= move;

   change= move_list[move_number + 1];
} ■
```

11.5 Second move computer analysis

Listing 11.5 presents the source code for the second_move_comp_analysis(...) function. This function examines the data in the program subconscious related to the current move list. It prepares the implementation of learning via the forced move algorithm by changing the last unforced move before a double threat setup by the computer. The only difference between this function and second_move_analysis(...) is that it considers Dr. Plopper's setup as opposed to the human's setup.

❏ **Listing 11.5** Source code for the second_move_comp_analysis(...) function.

```
//////////////////////////////////////
//
// void second_move_comp_analysis() does the level-two analysis
// by changing the last unforced move before a double threat is
// set up by the computer.
//
void second_move_comp_analysis()
{
int move;
   level= 2;
   move= moves_offset - 1;
   while( ( move_type_comp[move] != 1 ) ||
          ( move_type_comp[move-2] != 0 )  ){
      move= move - 2;
      }
   move= move - 1;
   while( ( move_type[move] == 1 ) ||
          ( move_type[move] == 3 ) ||
          ( move_list[move] == move_list[move + 1] ) ) {
      move= move - 2;
      }
   move_number= move;
   change= move_list[move_number + 1];
} ∎
```

11.6 Offensive first move analysis

Listing 11.6 presents the source code to the off_first_move_analysis(...) function. This function, which has been separated from the first_move_analysis(...) function to speed up the retrieval process, examines the data in the program subconscious related to the current move list. It prepares the implementation of learning via the forced move algorithm by changing the last unforced move before a loss, if Dr. Plopper moved first.

❑ **Listing 11.6** Source code for the off_first_move_analysis(...) function.

```
//////////////////////////////////////////////////////////////////
//
// void off_first_move_analysis() does the level-one analysis by
// changing the last unforced move before a loss, if Plopper makes
// the first move.
//
void off_first_move_analysis()
{
int move;

   end_move_flag= 0;

   level= 3;

   move= moves_offset - 2;

   if( move_type[move] == 9 ) {
      end_move_flag= 1;
      }
   while( ( move_type[move] == 1 ) ||
          ( move_type[move] == 3 ) ||
          ( move_list[move] == move_list[move + 1] ) ) {
     move= move - 2;
     if( move_type[move] == 9 ) {
        end_move_flag= 1;
        }
      }

   move_number= move;

   change= move_list[move_number + 1];
} ■
```

11.7 Offensive second move analysis

Listing 11.7 presents the source code to the off_second_move_analysis(...) function. This function examines the data in the program subconscious related to the current move list. It prepares the implementation of learning via the forced move algorithm by changing the last unforced move before a double threat setup is created by the human player, if Dr. Plopper moves first.

❑ **Listing 11.7**   Source code for the off_second_move_analysis(...) function.

```
//////////////////////////////////////////////////////////////
//
// void off_second_move_analysis() does the level-two analysis by
// changing the last unforced move before a double threat is
// set up by the human player, if Plopper makes the first move.
//

void off_second_move_analysis()
{
int move;

   level= 4;

   move= moves_offset - 1;

   while( ( move_type[move] != 1 ) ||
          ( move_type[move-2] != 0 ) ) {
      move= move - 2;
      }

   move= move-1;

   while( ( move_type[move] == 1 ) ||
          ( move_type[move] == 3 ) ||
          ( move_list[move] == move_list[move + 1] ) ) {
      move= move - 2;
      }

   move_number= move;

   change= move_list[move_number + 1];
}   ■
```

11.8 Offensive second move computer analysis

Listing 11.8 presents the source code to the off_second_move_comp_analysis(...) function. This function examines the data in the program subconscious related to the current move list. It prepares the implementation of learning via the forced move algorithm by changing the last unforced move before a double threat setup by the computer, if Dr. Plopper moves first.

❑ **Listing 11.8** Source code for the off_second_move_comp_analysis(...) function.

```
//////////////////////////////////////////////////////////////////
//
// void off_second_move_comp_analysis() does the level-two analysis
// by changing the last unforced move before a double threat is
// set up by the computer, if Plopper makes the first move.
//
void off_second_move_comp_analysis()
{
int move;

   level= 4;

   move= moves_offset - 1;

   while( ( move_type_comp[move] != 1 ) ||
          ( move_type_comp[move-2] !=0 ) ) {
     move= move - 2;
   }

   move= move - 1;

   while( ( move_type[move] == 1 ) ||
          ( move_type[move] == 3 ) ||
          ( move_list[move] == move_list[move + 1] ) ) {
     move= move - 2;
   }

   move_number= move;

   change= move_list[move_number + 1];
} ■
```

11.9 Implementation of marker disruption via `first_pat_analysis(...)`

Listing 11.9 presents the source code to the `first_pat_analysis(...)` function. This function represents the implementation of the marker disruption algorithm. It creates markers of primary and auxiliary patterns by first locating the coordinates of the "losing" and "auxiliary" squares. It then finds the other three squares that won the game. It does the same for the auxiliary square except that it searches for up to three patterns.

❏ **Listing 11.9** Source code for the `first_pat_analysis(...)` function.

```
///////////////////////////////////////////////
//
// void first_pat_analysis( UCHAR turn )
// creates the array of primary and auxiliary
// pattern by first locating the coordinates of
// the "losing" and "auxiliary" squares.  It
// then finds the three squares that won
// the game.  It does the same for the
// auxiliary square, except that it
// searches for up to three patterns.
//

void first_pat_analysis( UCHAR turn )
{
int loss_col,
    loss_row,
    aux_col,
    aux_row,
    temp_row,
    temp_col;

int total1,
    total2,
    found,
    real_flag= 0,
    ctr,
    acv= 0;

    level= 1;
    aux_flag= 0;
```

```
// Calculate and add loss & aux coordinates.

loss_col= move_list[moves_offset - 1];

loss_row= 8 - ( number_of_squares_in_column( loss_col ) );

aux_col= move_list[moves_offset - 2];

if( aux_col == loss_col ) {
   aux_row= 9 - ( number_of_squares_in_column( aux_col ) );
   }
else {
   aux_row= 8 - ( number_of_squares_in_column( aux_col ) );
   }

pat_list[acv++]= loss_row;
pat_list[acv++]= loss_col;
pat_list[acv++]= aux_row;
pat_list[acv++]= aux_col;

// Find the three real loss squares.

// Check East-West win.

found= FALSE;
total1= 0;
total2= 0;

// Check East.

if( ( loss_col < 7 ) &&
    ( !found ) ) {

   temp_row= loss_row;
   temp_col= loss_col + 1;

   for( ctr= 0; ctr < 3; ctr++ ) {
      if( ( temp_col < 8 ) &&
          ( board[temp_row][temp_col++] == turn ) ) {
         total1+= 1;
         }
      else {
         break;
         }
```

11.9 IMPLEMENTATION OF MARKER DISRUPTION VIA first_pat_analysis(...)

```
            if( total1 == 3 ) {
               found= TRUE;
               }
            }
         }
      }

   // Check West.

   if( ( loss_col > 0 ) &&
       ( !found ) ) {

      temp_row= loss_row;
      temp_col= loss_col - 1;

      for( ctr= 0; ctr < 3; ctr++ ) {
         if( ( temp_col >= 0 ) &&
             ( board[temp_row][temp_col--] == turn ) ) {
            total2+= 1;
            }
         else {
            break;
            }
         if( total2 + total1 == 3 ) {
            found= TRUE;
            break;
            }
         }
      }

   // Put "squares" into pattern array if found.

   if( ( found ) && ( !real_flag ) )  {

      real_flag= TRUE;

      for( ctr= 1; ctr <= total1; ctr++ ) {
         pat_list[acv++]= loss_row;
         pat_list[acv++]= loss_col + ctr;
         }

      for( ctr= 1; ctr <= total2; ctr++ ) {
         pat_list[acv++]= loss_row;
         pat_list[acv++]= loss_col - ctr;
         }
      }
```

```
// Check Northeast-Southwest win.

total1= 0;
total2= 0;

// Check Northeast.

if( ( loss_col < 7 ) &&
    ( loss_row > 0 ) &&
    ( !found ) ) {

   temp_row= loss_row - 1;
   temp_col= loss_col + 1;

   for( ctr= 0; ctr < 3; ctr++ ) {
      if( ( temp_col < 8 ) &&
          ( temp_row >= 0 ) &&
          ( board[temp_row--][temp_col++] == turn ) ) {
         total1+= 1;
         }
      else {
         break;
         }
      if( total1 == 3 ) {
         found= TRUE;
         }
      }
   }

// Check Southwest.

if( ( loss_col > 0 ) &&
    ( loss_row < 7 ) &&
    ( !found ) ) {

   temp_row= loss_row + 1;
   temp_col= loss_col - 1;

   for( ctr= 0; ctr < 3; ctr++ ) {
      if( ( temp_col >= 0 ) &&
          ( temp_row < 8 ) &&
          ( board[temp_row++][temp_col--] == turn ) ) {
         total2+= 1;
         }
```

11.9 IMPLEMENTATION OF MARKER DISRUPTION VIA first_pat_analysis(...)

```
         else {
            break;
            }
         if( total2 + total1 == 3 ) {
            found= TRUE;
            break;
            }
         }
      }

   // Put "squares" into pattern array if found.

   if( ( found ) && ( !real_flag ) ) {

      real_flag= TRUE;

      for( ctr= 1; ctr <= total1; ctr++ ) {
         pat_list[acv++]= loss_row - ctr;
         pat_list[acv++]= loss_col + ctr;
         }

      for( ctr= 1; ctr <= total2; ctr++ ) {
         pat_list[acv++]= loss_row + ctr;
         pat_list[acv++]= loss_col - ctr;
         }
      }

   // Check Southeast-Northwest Win.

   total1= 0;
   total2= 0;

   // Check Southeast.

   if( ( loss_col < 7 ) &&
       ( loss_row < 7 ) &&
       ( !found ) ) {

      temp_row= loss_row + 1;
      temp_col= loss_col + 1;
```

```
      for( ctr= 0; ctr < 3; ctr++ ) {
         if( ( temp_col < 8 ) &&
             ( temp_row < 8 ) &&
             ( board[temp_row++][temp_col++] == turn ) ) {
            total1+= 1;
            }
         else {
            break;
            }
         if( total1 == 3 ) {
            found= TRUE;
            }
         }
      }

   // Check Northwest.

   if( ( loss_col > 0 ) &&
       ( loss_row > 0 ) &&
       ( !found ) ) {

      temp_row= loss_row - 1;
      temp_col= loss_col - 1;

      for( ctr= 0; ctr < 3; ctr++ ) {
         if( ( temp_col >= 0 ) &&
             ( temp_row >= 0 ) &&
             ( board[temp_row--][temp_col--] == turn ) ) {
            total2+= 1;
            }
         else {
            break;
            }
         if( total2 + total1 == 3 ) {
            found= TRUE;
            break;
            }
         }
      }
```

11.9 IMPLEMENTATION OF MARKER DISRUPTION VIA first_pat_analysis(...)

```
   // Put "squares" into pattern array if found.

   if( ( found ) && ( !real_flag ) ) {

      real_flag= TRUE;

      for( ctr= 1; ctr <= total1; ctr++ ) {
         pat_list[acv++]= loss_row + ctr;
         pat_list[acv++]= loss_col + ctr;
         }

      for( ctr= 1; ctr <= total2; ctr++ ) {
         pat_list[acv++]= loss_row - ctr;
         pat_list[acv++]= loss_col - ctr;
         }
   }


// Find the three auxiliary loss squares.

// Check East-West Win.

found= FALSE;
total1= 0;
total2= 0;

// Check East.

if( aux_col < 7 ) {

   temp_row= aux_row;
   temp_col= aux_col + 1;

   for( ctr= 0; ctr < 3; ctr++ ) {
      if( ( temp_col < 8 ) &&
          ( board[temp_row][temp_col++] == turn ) ) {
         total1+= 1;
         }
      else {
         break;
         }
      if( total1 == 3 ) {
         found= TRUE;
         }
      }
   }
```

```
// Check West.

if( aux_col > 0 ) {

   temp_row= aux_row;
   temp_col= aux_col - 1;

   for( ctr= 0; ctr < 3; ctr++ ) {
      if( ( temp_col >= 0 ) &&
          ( board[temp_row][temp_col--] == turn ) ) {
         total2+= 1;
         }
      else {
         break;
         }
      if( total2 + total1 == 3 ) {
         found= TRUE;
         break;
         }
      }
   }

// Put "squares" into pattern array if found.

if( found ) {

   aux_flag= TRUE;

   for( ctr= 1; ctr <= total1; ctr++ ) {
      pat_list[acv++]= aux_row;
      pat_list[acv++]= aux_col + ctr;
      }

   for( ctr= 1; ctr <= total2; ctr++ ) {
      pat_list[acv++]= aux_row;
      pat_list[acv++]= aux_col - ctr;
      }
   }

// Check Northeast-Southwest win.

found= FALSE;
total1= 0;
total2= 0;
```

11.9 IMPLEMENTATION OF MARKER DISRUPTION VIA first_pat_analysis(...)

```
      // Check Southwest.
      if( ( aux_col > 0 ) &&
          ( aux_row < 7 ) ) {
         temp_row= aux_row + 1;
         temp_col= aux_col - 1;
         for( ctr= 0; ctr < 3; ctr++ ) {
            if( ( temp_col >= 0 ) &&
                ( temp_row < 8 ) &&
                ( board[temp_row++][temp_col--] == turn ) ) {
               total2+= 1;
               }
            else {
               break;
               }
            if( total2 + total1 == 3 ) {
               found= TRUE;
               break;
               }
            }
         }
      // Check Northeast.
      if( ( aux_col < 7 ) &&
          ( aux_row > 0 ) ) {
         temp_row= aux_row - 1;
         temp_col= aux_col + 1;
         for( ctr= 0; ctr < 3; ctr++ ) {
            if( ( temp_col < 8 ) &&
                ( temp_row >= 0 ) &&
                ( board[temp_row--][temp_col++] == turn ) ) {
               total1+= 1;
               }
            else {
               break;
               }
            if( total1 == 3 ) {
               found= TRUE;
               }
            }
         }
```

CHAPTER 11: PROGRAM LEARNING: ANALYZING A LOSS

```c
// Put "squares" into pattern array if found.

if( found ) {

   aux_flag= TRUE;

   for( ctr= 1; ctr <= total1; ctr++ ) {
      pat_list[acv++]= aux_row - ctr;
      pat_list[acv++]= aux_col + ctr;
      }

   for( ctr= 1; ctr <= total2; ctr++ ) {
      pat_list[acv++]= aux_row + ctr;
      pat_list[acv++]= aux_col - ctr;
      }
   }

// Check Southeast-Northwest win.

found= FALSE;
total1= 0;
total2= 0;

// Check Southeast.

if( ( aux_col < 7 ) &&
    ( aux_row < 7 ) ) {

   temp_row= aux_row + 1;
   temp_col= aux_col + 1;

   for( ctr= 0; ctr < 3; ctr++ ) {
      if( ( temp_col < 8 ) &&
          ( temp_row < 8 ) &&
          ( board[temp_row++][temp_col++] == turn ) ) {
         total1+= 1;
         }
      else {
         break;
         }
      if( total1 == 3 ) {
         found= TRUE;
         }
      }
   }
```

11.9 IMPLEMENTATION OF MARKER DISRUPTION VIA first_pat_analysis(...)

```
      // Check Northwest.

      if( ( aux_col > 0 ) &&
          ( aux_row > 0 ) ) {

         temp_row= aux_row - 1;
         temp_col= aux_col - 1;

         for( ctr= 0; ctr < 3; ctr++ ) {
            if( ( temp_col >= 0 ) &&
                ( temp_row >= 0 ) &&
                ( board[temp_row--][temp_col--] == turn ) ) {
               total2+= 1;
            }
            else {
               break;
            }
            if( total2 + total1 == 3 ) {
               found= TRUE;
               break;
            }
         }
      }

      // Put "squares" into pattern array if found.

      if( found ) {

         aux_flag= TRUE;

         for( ctr= 1; ctr <= total1; ctr++ ) {
            pat_list[acv++]= aux_row + ctr;
            pat_list[acv++]= aux_col + ctr;
         }

         for( ctr= 1; ctr <= total2; ctr++ ) {
            pat_list[acv++]= aux_row - ctr;
            pat_list[acv++]= aux_col - ctr;
         }
      }
```

```
      for ( ctr= 0; ctr < acv; ctr++ ) {
        if( ctr % 2 == 0 ) {
          pat_list2[ctr]= pat_list[ctr];
        }
        else {
          pat_list2[ctr]= 7 - pat_list[ctr];
        }
      }

} ∎
```

11.10 Adding a three-filled marker record and mirror to the program subconscious

Listing 11.10 presents the source code to the `add_pattern_list(...)` function. This function saves the level of pattern analysis, and the primary and auxiliary patterns into a marker in the program subconscious. It also creates a mirrored marker in the program subconscious, which doubles the power of the analysis.

❑ **Listing 11.10** Source code for the `add_pattern_list(...)` function.

```
///////////////////////////////////
//
// void add_pattern_list() saves
// the level of pattern analysis,
// and the primary and auxiliary
// patterns into a record in the
// array.  It also saves the mirrored
// record at the same time.
//

void add_pattern_list()
{
UCHAR *begin;
int   ctr;

   winpat_limit= WINPAT_SIZE / PAT_OFFSET;
```

11.10 ADDING A THREE-FILLED MARKER RECORD AND MIRROR

```
     if ( winpat_count > ( winpat_limit - 2 ) ) {
       return;
       }

     if ( !aux_flag ) {
       return;
       }

     // Increment record counter,
     // add original record.

     begin= ( winpat + ( winpat_count * PAT_OFFSET ) );

     *begin++= 1;

     *begin++= level;

     // movmem not supported by ICC,
     // movmem( pat_list, begin, PAT_OFFSET-2 );

     for( ctr= 0; ctr < PAT_OFFSET-2; ctr++ ) {
        *begin++= pat_list[ctr];
        }

     winpat_count += 1;

     // Add mirrored record.

     begin= ( winpat + ( winpat_count * PAT_OFFSET ) );

     *begin++= 1;

     *begin++= level;

     // movmem not supported by ICC,
     // movmem( pat_list2, begin, PAT_OFFSET-2 );

     for( ctr= 0; ctr < PAT_OFFSET - 2; ctr++ ) {
        *begin++= pat_list2[ctr];
        }

     winpat_count += 1;

} ■
```

11.11 Summary

Analysis of a loss takes place immediately after the loss occurs. The forced move and three-filled marker disruption algorithms guided the development of the analysis and learning functions. The functions developed from the forced move algorithm use the move sequence data to find the kiss of death move and alter it, so that the loss will not be repeated, and transfer a record of the analysis from the program conscious to the program subconscious. A similar process takes place for the three-filled marker disruption algorithm. The patterns of pieces around the place on the game board where the loss occurs are converted to memory markers and transferred from the program conscious to the program subconscious. These markers are scanned during game play. If Dr. Plopper notices that a marker associated with a loss appears to be being replicated, s/he will try to prevent it from being formed.

 *chapter 12*

Drop Four program learning: Implementation

The functions presented in this chapter are called during game play. They are used to access the records held in the program subconscious that are created immediately after a loss by the analysis functions presented in Chapter 9. These functions use information in the records held in the program subconscious to avoid repeating previously experienced losses. Losing game move sequences which will not be thwarted by the forced move algorithm are candidates for disruption by the three-filled marker disruption algorithm. Interestingly, a powerful synergy occurs when the forced move algorithm works in concert with the three-filled marker disruption algorithm. The program learning is truly powerful, and makes Drop Four a challenging, educational and fun game to play.

12.1 Finding winning patterns

The powerful find_winning_pattern(...) function searches the memory markers stored in the program subconscious until a partial match has been found. Once such a match has been found, a move that would disrupt the pattern is played. The second parameter of this function controls the number of pieces of the pattern that will be searched for: this is the *level* of board pattern recognition. Listing 12.1 presents the source code for the find_winning_pattern(...) function.

❑ **Listing 12.1**   Source code for the find_winning_pattern(...) function.

```
///////////////////////////////////////////////////////////////
//
// UCHAR find_winning_pattern(UCHAR turn, int pattern_start)
// searches the records until it finds one with a certain
// number of squares(pattern_start) that are filled with
// one color's(turn) pieces.  If it finds an applicable
// record, it finds which of the columns a piece can be
// placed in to further the pattern.  Then the column with
// the highest score in the evaluation array is returned.
//
UCHAR find_winning_pattern(UCHAR turn, int pattern_start)
{
int    lcv1,
       lcv2,
       lcv3,
       found= 0,
       total1,
       total2,
       acv;
UCHAR move, row, col, opponent;
UCHAR columns[8];
UCHAR first_ply[8]= { 0, 0, 0, 0, 0, 0, 0, 0 };
   if(turn == RED) {
      opponent= BLUE;
      }
   else {
      opponent= RED;
      }
   for(lcv1= 0; lcv1 < winpat_count ; lcv1++) {
      if ((winpat[(lcv1*PAT_OFFSET)]==1) &&
          (winpat[(lcv1*PAT_OFFSET) + 1]==1) &&
          (board[ (winpat[(lcv1*PAT_OFFSET) + (acv++)]) ]
          [ (winpat[(lcv1*PAT_OFFSET) + (acv++)]) ] != opponent) &&
          (board[ (winpat[(lcv1*PAT_OFFSET) + (acv++)]) ]
          [ (winpat[(lcv1*PAT_OFFSET) + (acv++)]) ] != opponent)) {
```

12.1 FINDING WINNING PATTERNS

```
          acv= 6;
          total1= 0;
          for(lcv2= 0; lcv2 < 3; lcv2++) {
             row= winpat[(lcv1*PAT_OFFSET) + (acv++)];
             col= winpat[(lcv1*PAT_OFFSET) + (acv++)];
             if (board[row][col]==turn) {
                ++total1;
                }
             if (board[row][col]==opponent) {
                --total1;
                }
             }
          for(lcv2= 1; lcv2 < 4; lcv2++) {
             total2= 0;
             for(lcv3= 0; lcv3 < 3; lcv3++) {
                row= winpat[(lcv1*PAT_OFFSET) + (acv++)];
                col= winpat[(lcv1*PAT_OFFSET) + (acv++)];
                if (board[row][col]==turn) {
                   ++total2;
                   }
                if (board[row][col]==opponent) {
                   --total2;
                   }
                }
             if (total1 + total2 >= pattern_start) {
                found= TRUE;
                record= lcv1;
                subrecord= lcv2;
                }
             }
          if (found) {
             break;
             }
          }
       }

   if (found) {
      for (lcv1= 0; lcv1 < 8; lcv1++) {
         columns[lcv1]= number_of_squares_in_column((UCHAR)lcv1);
         }
```

```
      acv= 6;
      for(lcv2= 0; lcv2 < 3; lcv2++) {
         row= winpat[(record*PAT_OFFSET) + (acv++)];
         col= winpat[(record*PAT_OFFSET) + (acv++)];
         if((columns[col] == 7 - row) &&
            (coffin[col] != 1) &&
            (coffin[col] != 3)) {
           first_ply[col]= 1;
         }
      }
      acv= 6;
      for(lcv2= 0; lcv2 < 3; lcv2++) {
         row= winpat[(record*PAT_OFFSET) + (6*subrecord) + (acv++)];
         col= winpat[(record*PAT_OFFSET) + (6*subrecord) + (acv++)];
         if((columns[col] == 7 - row) &&
            (coffin[col] != 1) &&
            (coffin[col] != 3)) {
           first_ply[col]= 1;
         }
      }

   }

   move= first_ply_move(turn, first_ply);
   if(move != NO_FIRST_PLY_MOVE) {
     return move;
    }

   return NO_WINNING_PATTERN;
} ■
```

12.2 Learning is demonstrated via `first_move_check(...)`

The `first_move_check(...)` function presented in Listing 12.2 is a key implementation of the OAI paradigm. This function searches through the program subconscious for the point in a level-one analysis which, in effect, is the memory of a previously experienced move sequence. If such a sequence is identified, Dr. Plopper looks at the analysis of the loss, and returns a stronger move than the one generated via program instinct.

Listing 12.2 Source code for the first_move_check(...) function.

```
////////////////////////////////////////////
//
// UCHAR first_move_check( UCHAR moves_offset )
// searches through the records until it finds
// a level-one analysis that needs a change
// at this move ( moves_offset ), and has
// the same sequence up to this point.  If it
// finds one, it returns the changed move.
//

UCHAR first_move_check( UCHAR moves_offset )
{
int    lcv1, lcv2, found;
UCHAR move;

   for( lcv1= 0; lcv1 < winmov_count ; lcv1++ ) {
      if( ( winmov[( lcv1*MOVE_OFFSET )] == 1 ) &&
          ( winmov[( lcv1*MOVE_OFFSET ) + 1] == 1 ) &&
          ( winmov[( lcv1*MOVE_OFFSET ) + 2] == moves_offset ) ) {
         found= 1;
         for( lcv2= 0; lcv2 < moves_offset; lcv2++ ) {
            if( move_list[lcv2] !=
                winmov[( lcv1*MOVE_OFFSET ) + lcv2 + 4] ) {
              found= 0;
              break;
              }
            }
         if( found ) {
           move= winmov[( lcv1 * MOVE_OFFSET ) + 3];
           record= lcv1;
           return move;
           }
         }
      }
   return NO_MATCHING_RECORD;
}
```

12.3 Learning is demonstrated via `second_move_check(...)`

Listing 12.3 presents the source code to the `second_move_check(...)` function. This searches through the program subconscious to look for the place in a level-two analysis record which has previously been stored and returns a more adaptive move that the one returned during the loss.

❏ **Listing 12.3** Source code for the `second_move_check(...)` function.

```
/////////////////////////////////////////////////
//
// UCHAR second_move_check( UCHAR moves_offset )
// searches through the records until it finds
// a level-two analysis that needs a change
// at this move ( moves_offset ), and has
// the same sequence up to this point.  If it
// finds one, it returns the changed move.
//

UCHAR second_move_check( UCHAR moves_offset )
{
int    lcv1, lcv2, found;
UCHAR move;

    for( lcv1= 0; lcv1 < winmov_count ; lcv1++ ) {
       if( ( winmov[( lcv1*MOVE_OFFSET )] == 1 ) &&
           ( winmov[( lcv1*MOVE_OFFSET ) + 1] == 2 ) &&
           ( winmov[( lcv1*MOVE_OFFSET ) + 2] ==
              moves_offset ) ) {
          found= 1;
          for( lcv2= 0; lcv2 < moves_offset; lcv2++ ) {
             if( move_list[lcv2] !=
                 winmov[( lcv1 * MOVE_OFFSET ) + lcv2 + 4] ) {
                found= 0;
                break;
             }
          }
```

12.4 LEARNING IS DEMONSTRATED VIA first_human_win(...)

```
        if( found ) {
          move= winmov[( lcv1 * MOVE_OFFSET ) + 3];
          if ( coffin[move] != 1 ) {
            record= lcv1;
            return move;
          }
        }
      }
    }
  return NO_MATCHING_RECORD;
}
```

12.4 Learning is demonstrated via first_human_win(...)

The first_human_win(...) function presented in Listing 12.4 implements an offensive move based on program learning. This searches through a previously developed level-one analysis and seeks to create the trap that had originally defeated Dr. Plopper. This powerful function facilitates Dr. Plopper's learning from a human's skillful play and using that play against other humans. Quite cool.

❑ **Listing 12.4** Source code for the first_human_win(...) function.

```
///////////////////////////////////////////////
//
// UCHAR first_human_win( UCHAR moves_offset )
// is the function that Plopper uses when it
// goes first, to search for an applicable
// level-one record that was created in a
// game when it made the second move.  If the
// sequences match up to a certain point, then
// the function returns a move that creates the
// trap that originally defeated Plopper.
//

UCHAR first_human_win( UCHAR moves_offset )
{
int    lcv1, lcv2, found;
UCHAR move;
```

```
        for( lcv1= 0; lcv1 < winmov_count ; lcv1++ ) {
           if( ( winmov[( lcv1*MOVE_OFFSET )] == 1 ) &&
               ( winmov[( lcv1*MOVE_OFFSET ) + 1] == 1 ) &&
               ( winmov[( lcv1*MOVE_OFFSET ) + 2] <=
                 moves_offset + 1 ) ) {
              found= 1;
              for( lcv2= 0; lcv2 < moves_offset; lcv2++ ) {
                 if( lcv2 !=
                     winmov[( lcv1 * MOVE_OFFSET ) + 3] ) {
                    if( move_list[lcv2] !=
                        winmov[( lcv1 * MOVE_OFFSET ) + lcv2 + 4] ) {
                       found= 0;
                       break;
                    }
                 }
                 else {
                   if ( move_list[lcv2] ==
                        winmov[( lcv1*MOVE_OFFSET ) + 3] ) {
                      found= 0;
                      break;
                   }
                 }

              }
              if ( found ) {
                move= winmov[( lcv1*MOVE_OFFSET ) + 4 + moves_offset];
                record= lcv1;
                return move;
              }
           }
        }
        return NO_HUMAN_WIN;
     } ∎
```

12.5 Learning is demonstrated via second_human_win(...)

Listing 12.5 presents the source code to the second_human_win(...) offensive program learning–based function. This searches through a previously developed level-two analysis and seeks to create the trap that originally defeated Dr. Plopper. This powerful

12.5 LEARNING IS DEMONSTRATED VIA second_human_win(...)

function facilitates Dr. Plopper's learning from a human's skillful play and using that play against other humans.

❑ **Listing 12.5** Source code for the `second_human_win(...)` function.

```
//////////////////////////////////////////////////
//
// UCHAR second_human_win( UCHAR moves_offset ) is the
// function that Plopper uses when it goes first, to
// search for an applicable level-two record that was
// created in agame when it made the second move.  If
// the sequences match up to a certain point, then the
// function returns a move that creates the trap that
// originally defeated Plopper.
//

UCHAR second_human_win( UCHAR moves_offset )
{
int    lcv1, lcv2, found;
UCHAR move;

    for( lcv1= 0; lcv1 < winmov_count ; lcv1++ ) {
        if( ( winmov[( lcv1*MOVE_OFFSET )] == 1 ) &&
            ( winmov[( lcv1*MOVE_OFFSET ) + 1] == 2 ) &&
            ( winmov[( lcv1*MOVE_OFFSET ) + 2] <=
              moves_offset + 1 ) ) {
            found= 1;
            for( lcv2= 0; lcv2 < moves_offset ; lcv2++ ) {
                if(   lcv2 !=
                      winmov[( lcv1*MOVE_OFFSET ) + 2] ) {
                  if( move_list[lcv2] !=
                      winmov[( lcv1*MOVE_OFFSET ) + lcv2 + 4] ) {
                      found= 0;
                      break;
                      }
                }
                else {
                  if ( move_list[lcv2] ==
                      winmov[( lcv1*MOVE_OFFSET ) + 3] ) {
                      found= 0;
                      break;
                      }
                }
            }
```

```
            if ( found ) {
              move= winmov[( lcv1*MOVE_OFFSET ) + 4 + moves_offset];
              record= lcv1;
              return move;
            }
          }
       }
   return NO_HUMAN_WIN;
} ■
```

12.6 Learning is demonstrated via off_first_human_win(...)

Listing 12.6 presents the source code to the off_first_human_win(...) function. This function demonstrates program learning when Dr. Plopper moves second. It searches through a previously developed level-one analysis and seeks to create the trap that had originally defeated Dr. Plopper. This powerful function facilitates Dr. Plopper's learning from a human's skillful play and using that play against other humans.

❑ **Listing 12.6** Source code for the off_first_human_win(...) function.

```
///////////////////////////////////////////////////
//
// UCHAR off_first_human_win( UCHAR moves_offset )
// is the function that Plopper uses when it
// goes second, to search for an applicable
// level-one record that was created in a
// game when it made the first move.  If the
// sequences match up to a certain point, then
// the function returns a move that creates the
// trap that originally defeated Plopper.
//

UCHAR off_first_human_win( UCHAR moves_offset )
{
int    lcv1, lcv2, found;
UCHAR  move;
```

```
for( lcv1= 0; lcv1 < winmov_count ; lcv1++ ) {
   if( ( winmov[( lcv1*MOVE_OFFSET )] == 1 ) &&
       ( winmov[( lcv1*MOVE_OFFSET ) + 1] == 3 ) &&
       ( winmov[( lcv1*MOVE_OFFSET ) + 2] <=
         moves_offset + 1 ) ) {
      found= 1;
      for( lcv2= 0; lcv2 < moves_offset ; lcv2++ ) {
         if (   lcv2 !=
                winmov[( lcv1*MOVE_OFFSET ) + 3] ) {
            if ( move_list[lcv2] !=
                 winmov[( lcv1*MOVE_OFFSET ) + lcv2 + 4] ) {
               found= 0;
               break;
            }
         }
         else {
            if ( move_list[lcv2] ==
                 winmov[( lcv1*MOVE_OFFSET ) + 3] ) {
               found= 0;
               break;
            }
         }

      }
      if ( found ) {
        move= winmov[( lcv1*MOVE_OFFSET ) + 4 + moves_offset];
        record= lcv1;
        return move;
      }
   }
}
return NO_HUMAN_WIN;
}
```

12.7 Learning is demonstrated via `off_second_human_win(...)`

Listing 12.7 presents the source code to the `off_second_human_win(...)` function. This function demonstrates program learning when Dr. Plopper moves second. This searches through a previously developed level-two analysis and seeks to create the trap that had originally defeated Dr. Plopper. This powerful function facilitates Dr. Plopper's learning from a human's skillful play and using that play against other humans.

❏ **Listing 12.7** Source code for the off_second_human_win(...) function.

```
///////////////////////////////////////////////////////////////
//
// UCHAR off_second_human_win( UCHAR moves_offset ) is the function
// that Plopper uses when it goes second, to search for an applicable
// level-two record that was created in a game when it made the first
// move.  If the sequences match up to a certain point, the functions
// return a move that creates the trap that originally defeated Plopper.
//

UCHAR off_second_human_win( UCHAR moves_offset )
{
int    lcv1, lcv2, found;
UCHAR move;

   for( lcv1= 0; lcv1 < winmov_count ; lcv1++ ) {
      if( ( winmov[( lcv1*MOVE_OFFSET )] == 1 ) &&
          ( winmov[( lcv1*MOVE_OFFSET ) + 1] == 4 ) &&
          ( winmov[( lcv1*MOVE_OFFSET ) + 2] <=
            moves_offset + 1 ) ) {
         found= 1;
         for( lcv2= 0; lcv2 < moves_offset ; lcv2++ ) {
            if( lcv2 !=
                winmov[( lcv1*MOVE_OFFSET ) + 2] ) {
               if( move_list[lcv2] !=
                   winmov[( lcv1*MOVE_OFFSET ) + lcv2 + 4] ) {
                 found= 0;
                 break;
               }
            }
            else {
               if( move_list[lcv2] ==
                   winmov[( lcv1*MOVE_OFFSET ) + 3] ) {
                 found= 0;
                 break;
               }
            }

         }
```

```
              if ( found ) {
                move= winmov[( lcv1*MOVE_OFFSET ) + 4 + moves_offset];
                record= lcv1;
                return move;
                }
            }
         }
      return NO_HUMAN_WIN;
   }
```

12.8 The `off_first_move_check(...)` function

Listing 12.8 presents the source code to the `off_first_move_check(...)` function. This function searches through sequence records in the program subconscious until it finds a matching level-one sequence. If the match is found and Dr. Plopper had made the first move, it returns the "learned" move, which was identified during the analysis after the loss.

❏ **Listing 12.8**   Source code for the `off_first_move_check(...)` function.

```
/////////////////////////////////////////////////////
//
// UCHAR off_first_move_check( UCHAR moves_offset )
// searches through the records until it finds a
// matching level-one record, if Plopper makes the
// first move.  If it finds one, it returns
// the changed move.
//

UCHAR off_first_move_check( UCHAR moves_offset )
{
int    lcv1, lcv2, found;
UCHAR move;

   for( lcv1= 0; lcv1 < winmov_count; lcv1++ ) {
      if( ( winmov[( lcv1 * MOVE_OFFSET )] == 1 ) &&
          ( winmov[( lcv1 * MOVE_OFFSET ) + 1] == 3 ) &&
          ( winmov[( lcv1 * MOVE_OFFSET ) + 2] ==
            moves_offset ) ) {
```

```
            found= 1;

            for( lcv2= 0; lcv2 < moves_offset; lcv2++ ) {
               if( move_list[lcv2] !=
                   winmov[( lcv1 * MOVE_OFFSET ) + lcv2 + 4] ) {
                  found= 0;
                  break;
               }
            }

            if( found ) {
               move= winmov[( lcv1 * MOVE_OFFSET ) + 3];
               record= lcv1;
               return move;
            }
         }
      }

      return NO_MATCHING_RECORD;
   } ∎
```

12.9 The off_second_move_check(...) *function*

Listing 12.9 presents the source code to the off_second_move_check(...) function. This function searches through sequence records in the program subconscious until it finds a matching level-two sequence. If a match is found and Dr. Plopper had made the first move, it returns the "learned" move, which was identified during the analysis after the loss.

❏ **Listing 12.9** Source code for the off_second_move_check(...) function.

```
///////////////////////////////////////////////
//
// UCHAR off_second_move_check( UCHAR moves_offset )
// searches through the records until it finds a
// matching level-two record, if Plopper makes the
// first move.  If it finds one, it returns
// the changed move.
//
```

```
UCHAR off_second_move_check( UCHAR moves_offset )
{
int    lcv1, lcv2, found;
UCHAR move;

    for( lcv1= 0; lcv1 < winmov_count ; lcv1++ ) {
        if( ( winmov[( lcv1*MOVE_OFFSET )] == 1 ) &&
            ( winmov[( lcv1*MOVE_OFFSET ) + 1] == 4 ) &&
            ( winmov[( lcv1*MOVE_OFFSET ) + 2] ==
              moves_offset ) ) {
          found= 1;
          for( lcv2= 0; lcv2 < moves_offset; lcv2++ ) {
              if( move_list[lcv2] !=
                  winmov[( lcv1 * MOVE_OFFSET ) + lcv2 + 4] ) {
                found= 0;
                break;
              }
          }
          if( found ) {
            move= winmov[( lcv1 * MOVE_OFFSET ) + 3];
            if( coffin[move] != 1 ) {
              record= lcv1;
              return move;
            }
          }
        }
    }
    return NO_MATCHING_RECORD;
} ■
```

12.10 Summary

This chapter presented the functions which implement program learning using the results of the analysis functions presented in Chapter 11. The analysis and implementation functions were developed using the OAI paradigm as a guide, and work together hand-in-hand.

chapter 13

Transferring the program subconscious to and from disk and RAM

We have saved the simplest and most trivial chapter for last. This chapter contains the source code to two simple I/O functions. They involve reading data from and writing data to the hard disk via standard C I/O functions. Conforming with the OAI paradigm, the data transfers to and from the program subconscious take place at the very beginning of Drop Four's program execution and just before its termination.

Note that we used C's fopen(...), f..., etc., calls to facilitate the port to different operating systems and compilers. Currently we have compiled the engine7.c source file (where the source to open_data_base(...) and close_data_base(...) is located) using Borland's C++ for DOS, Borland's C++ for OS/2, IBM's CSET++ for OS/2, and MetaWare's High C/C++ for OS/2, with no trouble at all.

13.1 Transferring the program subconscious from hard disk to RAM

Listing 13.1 presents the source code to the open_data_base(...) function. This function is called shortly after Drop Four's main() function is called. The information contained in the program subconscious held on hard disk is automatically transferred to the program subconscious held in RAM.

❏ **Listing 13.1** Source code for the `open_data_base(...)` function.

```
/////////////////////////////////
//
// void open_data_base() reads
// the array and number of
// records from the data files
// winmov.dat and winpat.dat.
//

void open_data_base()
{
FILE *in, *out;

   memset(winpat, WINPAT_SIZE, 0);
   memset(winmov, WINMOV_SIZE, 0);
   memset(new_sequences, SEQ_SIZE, 0);
   memset(endmov, ENDMOV_SIZE, 0);
   memset(humanmov, HUMANMOV_SIZE, 0);

   current.new_win= 0;
   current.new_loss= 0;
   current.new_draw= 0;
   current.beg_win= 0;
   current.beg_loss= 0;
   current.beg_draw= 0;
   current.int_win= 0;
   current.int_loss= 0;
   current.int_draw= 0;
   current.adv_win= 0;
   current.adv_loss= 0;
   current.adv_draw= 0;

   in= fopen("winmov.dat","rb+");
   if(in != NULL) {
      fread(&winmov_count, 2, 1, in);
      fread(winmov, WINMOV_SIZE, 1, in);
      fclose(in);
      }
```

13.1 TRANSFERRING THE PROGRAM SUBCONSCIOUS FROM HARD DISK

```
   in= fopen("winpat.dat","rb+");
   if(in != NULL) {
      fread(&winpat_count, 2, 1, in);
      fread(winpat, WINPAT_SIZE, 1, in);
      fclose(in);
      }
   in= fopen("sequence.dat","rb+");
   if(in != NULL) {
      fread(&sequence_count, 2, 1, in);
      fread(new_sequences, SEQ_SIZE, 1, in);
      fclose(in);
      }
   in= fopen("endmov.dat","rb+");
   if(in != NULL) {
      fread(&endmov_count, 2, 1, in);
      fread(endmov, ENDMOV_SIZE, 1, in);
      fclose(in);
      }
   in= fopen("stats.dat","rb+");
   if(in != NULL) {
      fread(&current.new_win, 3, 1, in);
      fread(&current.new_loss, 3, 1, in);
      fread(&current.new_draw, 3, 1, in);
      fread(&current.beg_win, 3, 1, in);
      fread(&current.beg_loss, 3, 1, in);
      fread(&current.beg_draw, 3, 1, in);
      fread(&current.int_win, 3, 1, in);
      fread(&current.int_loss, 3, 1, in);
      fread(&current.int_draw, 3, 1, in);
      fread(&current.adv_win, 3, 1, in);
      fread(&current.adv_loss, 3, 1, in);
      fread(&current.adv_draw, 3, 1, in);
      fclose(in);
      }
  in= fopen("humanmov.dat","rb+");
  if(in != NULL) {
      fread(&humanmov_count, 2, 1, in);
      fread(humanmov, HUMANMOV_SIZE, 1, in);
      fclose(in);
      }
} ∎
```

13.2 Transferring the program subconscious from RAM to hard disk

Listing 13.2 presents the source code to the `close_data_base(...)` function. This function is called shortly before completing execution of Drop Four's `main()` function. Once the `main()` function is completed, Drop Four will return control to the operating system. The information contained in the program subconscious held in RAM is automatically transferred to the program subconscious held on hard disk.

❑ **Listing 13.2** Source code for the `close_data_base(...)` function.

```
/////////////////////////////////////
//
// void close_data_base() rewrites the
// updated array and number of records
// to the data files winmov.dat and winpat.dat.
//

void close_data_base()
{
FILE *in, *out;

   in= fopen("winmov.dat","wb+");
   fwrite(&winmov_count, 2, 1, in);
   fwrite(winmov, WINMOV_SIZE, 1, in);
   fclose(in);

   in= fopen("winpat.dat","wb+");
   fwrite(&winpat_count, 2, 1, in);
   fwrite(winpat, WINPAT_SIZE, 1, in);
   fclose(in);

   in= fopen("sequence.dat","wb+");
   fwrite(&sequence_count, 2, 1, in);
   fwrite(new_sequences, SEQ_SIZE, 1, in);
   fclose(in);

   in= fopen("stats.dat","wb+");
   fwrite(&current.new_win, 3, 1, in);
   fwrite(&current.new_loss, 3, 1, in);
   fwrite(&current.new_draw, 3, 1, in);
```

```
      fwrite(&current.beg_win, 3, 1, in);
      fwrite(&current.beg_loss, 3, 1, in);
      fwrite(&current.beg_draw, 3, 1, in);
      fwrite(&current.int_win, 3, 1, in);
      fwrite(&current.int_loss, 3, 1, in);
      fwrite(&current.int_draw, 3, 1, in);
      fwrite(&current.adv_win, 3, 1, in);
      fwrite(&current.adv_loss, 3, 1, in);
      fwrite(&current.adv_draw, 3, 1, in);
      fclose(in);

}   ■
```

13.3 Summary

This short final chapter demonstrated how to transfer data contained in the program subconscious on hard disk to the program subconscious in RAM, and vice versa, via standard C I/O functions. Nothing mysterious here. The only caveat is that to conform to the OAI paradigm we call the `open_data_base(...)` function very early in Drop Four's `main()` function execution, and call the `close_data_base(...)` function just before termination of Drop Four's `main()` function.

epilogue

Objective artificial intelligence is a high-level paradigm that we have developed to facilitate the creation of algorithms for use in implementing programs which clearly demonstrate learning. We believe that programs which can learn from their mistakes are better than those that can't. The OAI paradigm has been drawn from the fields of psychology, philosophy, and computer science. *Program instinct* and *program learning* are terms which refer to two distinct methods that a program can use to generate a response. Program instinct refers to the program's ability to respond to input without any prior experience. Program learning, on the other hand, refers to the ability of the program to learn from the consequences of previous experiences, in particular, to avoid the negative consequences that have been previously experienced. One powerful feature of program learning is the ability to make an abstraction from the original data analysis to increase the scope of the impact of learning. This was accomplished in Drop Four by creating symmetrical data of sequence-related move lists and piece patterns surrounding losses (markers). The learning from a single loss is applied to offensive and defensive situations, whether Dr. Plopper moves first or second.

Three algorithms developed from the OAI paradigm were presented in the book. The first and simplest was the move elimination algorithm. This algorithm simply removes a move from a list of potential moves if a loss has previously been experienced using it. The second learning algorithm presented was the forced move algorithm. Here, the record of game moves is examined backwards from the last move to determine the last move that wasn't forced. That move is then changed. Unfortunately, the forced move algorithm is not robust enough to handle all of the winning games that a human may manage to create.

From the ashes of the forced move algorithm, the three-filled marker disruption algorithm was born. Here, we developed a pattern recognition function that is able to determine when different levels of undesirable patterns are being created by the human. Once the three-filled marker disruption algorithm determines that a dangerous pattern is indeed being formed, it actively moves to disrupt the formation of the complete pattern. In addition, this algorithm can be used to bolster offensive strategies by getting the program to seek the creation of its own patterns.

This book has been the culmination of countless (okay, Len can be prone to exaggeration) hours of reading, productive discussion, arguing, and coding. The intellectual exercise culminated in the development of Drop Four. Like the OAI paradigm or not, using it helped us to develop Drop Four's single loss learning along with its ability to make moves quickly. This last feature proves highly valuable for use in game design.

It is our hope that this work sets the groundwork for the development of additional OAI-based algorithms that provide the facility for a computer program to demonstrate the ability to learn in specialized situations. We don't want to debate whether that's how consciousness or the brain works; we're simply interested in demonstrating computers can learn and respond in many situations as a human might. No more, no less.

Finally, we'd love to know of any OAI-based implementations you come up with. You can reach us on the internet at `ldorfman@li.net`. *Namaste'*.

index

A

`add_list(...)` function   229–231
`add_pattern_list(...)` function   250–251
artificial intelligence, objective.   *See* objective artificial intelligence
awareness, definition   3

B

balance, program learning and program instinct   60

C

`check_for_loss(...)` function   155–157
`check_for_pattern(...)` function   203–205
`check_for_win(...)` function   154–155
`close_data_base(...)` function   272–273
`coffin[]` array, role in move generation in Drop Four   101–114
`coffin_corner( UCHAR turn )` function   113
`coffin_pattern(turn)` function   111–112

consciousness models, human and computer   2–5, 7, 12
`create_coffin(...)` function   105–107
`create_coffin_o(opponent)` function   108–109
`create_setup2(...)` function   157–159
`create_win_board()` function   110–111

D

disk access functions   269–273
`do_positional_move(...)` function   166–167
double wins   150
Drop Four (game).   *See also* forced move algorithm
  adding a move to the move list   229–231
  `coffin[]` array, role in move generation   101–114
  double wins, determining   150
  `evaluation_first_ply[8]` array   206
  first-move selection   115–143, 231–236

Drop Four *(continued)*
  function map   75–80
  functions. *See* functions
  getting number of pieces in a game board column   149
  implementation overview   52–59, 70
  initializing ghost boards   148
  level-two analysis support function   233
  levels of play   116–118
  marker disruption implementation 239–250
  move generation, basic concepts 101–114
  move generation, positional   201–227
  move selection implementation   73–100
  move selection sequence design   68–69
  option settings for game play   80–86
  overview and analysis   49–60
  pattern matching   165–199
  ply searching   145–163
  positional moves, non-ply   166–199
  program learning   1–2, 70–71, 229–267
  `raw_score` array   206
  relocating data between boards   148–149
  searching for wins   152–155
  second move computer analysis   235
  three-filled patterns   202–205
  `weights[8]` array   206
  wins on ghost boards, determining   151

E
`evaluate_board(...)` function   205–227
`evaluation_first_ply[8]` array   206

F
`find_winning_pattern(...)` function 253–256
first-move analysis in Drop Four game 231–236
`first_human_win(...)` function   259–260

`first_move_analysis(...)` function 231–232
`first_move_check(...)` function   256–257
`first_pat_analysis(...)` function   239–250
`first_ply_move(...)` function   205–207
forced move algorithm. *See also* program learning; objective artificial intelligence
  coding   16–28
  conditions for failure   13
  conditions for success   53
  synergy with three-filled marker disruption algorithm   253
  theoretical basis   63–65, 70–71
  use   100, 229, 231, 237
forced move, definition   15, 63
forced-win search   157–159
forks, blocking   161–163
four-in-a-row games   50.   *See also* Drop Four function
  `add_list(...)`   229–231
  `add_pattern_list(...)`   250–251
  `check_for_loss(...)`   155–157
  `check_for_pattern(...)`   203–205
  `check_for_win(...)`   154–155
  `close_data_base(...)`   272–273
  `coffin_corner( UCHAR turn )`   113
  `coffin_pattern(turn)`   111–112
  `create_coffin(...)`   105–107
  `create_coffin_o(opponent)`   108–109
  `create_setup2(...)`   157–159
  `create_win_board()`   110–111
  determining double wins   150
  determining wins on ghost boards   151
  disk access   269–273
  `do_positional_move(...)`   166–167
  `evaluate_board(...)`   205–227
  `find_winning_pattern(...)`   253–256
  `first_human_win(...)`   259–260
  `first_move_analysis(...)`   231–232
  `first_move_check(...)`   256–257
  `first_pat_analysis(...)`   239–250
  `first_ply_move(...)`   205–207

INDEX   279

`get_computer_move(...)`   115
`get_computer_move_first(...)`   115–143
getting number of pieces in column   149

`init_coffin()`   105
initializing ghost boards   148
input/output   269–273
`look_ahead_opp(...)`   161–163
map   75–80
`off_first_human_win(...)`   262–263
`off_first_move_analysis(...)`   236
`off_first_move_check(...)`   265–266
`off_second_human_win(...)`   263–265
`off_second_move_analysis(...)`   237
`off_second_move_check(...)`   266–267
`off_second_move_comp_analysis(...)`   238
`open_data_base(...)`   269–271
`opening_book_defensive(...)`   171–190
`opening_book_first(...)`   167–170
`opening_book_offensive(...)`   191–199
`opponent_type_move(...)`   233
`pattern_search_board(...)`   202
ply search   145–163
relocating data between boards   148–149
searching for wins   152–155
`second_human_win(...)`   260–262
`second_move_analysis(...)`   234
`second_move_check(...)`   258–259
`second_move_comp_analysis(...)`   235
`start_game(...)`   86–99
`stop_setup2(...)`   159–161

G

game design.   *See* Drop Four; Tic Tac Toe
`get_computer_move(...)` function   115
`get_computer_move_first(...)` function   115–143
ghost boards   146–155, 203

H

human consciousness, model   2–4

I

`init_coffin()` function   105
initializing ghost boards   148
input/output functions   269–273
instinct, program.   *See* program instinct

K

kiss of death move theory   63–65, 229

L

learning, program.   *See* program learning
level-two analysis support function   233
`look_ahead_opp(...)` function   161–163
loss analysis   229–267

M

marker disruption   53, 71, 239–250
memory
 definitions   2
 markers   2, 5–6, 66–67, 229
 role in program learning   1
move elimination algorithm   13, 31–47.
 See also objective artificial intelligence
move generation   201–227

O

objective artificial intelligence
 analysis   11, 14–15, 53–59
 definition   1–2, 6
 design overview   11–12, 15–16, 61–72
 implementation overview   9–16, 52–59
 problem statement   10–11, 14, 52
 suitability for application   7–9, 14, 51–52

280 INDEX

off_first_human_win(...) function 262–263
off_first_move_analysis(...) function 236
off_first_move_check(...) function 265
off_second_human_win(...) function 263–265
off_second_move_analysis(...) function 237
off_second_move_check(...) function 266
off_second_move_comp_analysis(...) function 238
open_data_base(...) function 269–271
opening book moves in game design 167–199
opening_book_defensive(...) function 171–190
opening_book_first(...) function 167–170
opening_book_offensive(...) function 191–199
opponent_type_move(...) function 233

P

pattern analysis after game completion 229
pattern recognition and matching 71, 165–199, 202–203, 239–256
pattern_search_board(...) function 202
ply searching 145–163
position evaluation in board game theory 201–102, 205–227
positional moves in game design 166–199
program consciousness 4–5, 7, 12
program instinct
    basic concepts 101–114
    coffin[] array 101–114
    definition 7
    design and implementation 29–31, 54–59, 69–70
    move decision scheme 115–143
    non-ply positional moves 166–199
    opening book defensive moves 171–190
    opening book offensive moves 191–199
    pattern matching 165–199
    ply searching 145–163
    positional move generation 201–227
    purpose 13

program learning. *See also* objective artificial intelligence; forced move algorithm; marker disruption algorithm; move elimination algorithm
    analyzing a loss 229–252
    definition 7
    design principles in Drop Four 70–71
    effectiveness in Drop Four 1–2
    implementation in Drop Four 253–267
    role of memory 1
programming environment and tools 67

R

raw_score array 206

S

second-move analysis in Drop Four 231–236, 238
second_human_win(...) function 260–262
second_move_analysis(...) function 234
second_move_check(...) function 258–259
second_move_comp_analysis(...) 235
start_game(...) function 86–99
stop_setup2(...) function 159–161
subconsciousness, computer 5, 12

T

three-filled marker disruption algorithm 71, 100, 253. *See also* objective artificial intelligence; program learning
three-filled patterns 202–205, 250–251
Tic Tac Toe 13–48

U

unconsciousness, computer 5, 12

W

weights[8] array 206
win_board array 110–111

Diskette contents

The diskette accompanying the book contains the following directories:

- `\src` contains the source code to the Drop Four game. The executable is labeled `game.exe`. We used Borland's C/C++ compiler 4.0. You can make `game.exe` with Borland's `make.exe` utility program.
- `\ttt1` contains the source code to Chapter 4's Tic Tac Toe, version 1.
- `\ttt2` contains the source code to Chapter 4's Tic Tac Toe, version 2.
- `\ttt3` contains the source code to Chapter 4's Tic Tac Toe, version 3.

Drop Four directions

1. Set the game play level to advanced if you wish to see learning take place.
2. Begin play by selecting the Start option. A left button click on Start will begin the game.
3. Select a move by clicking once on the button above the column.
4. Drop Four will notify you when the game is over. Click on Start to begin a new game.
5. If you wish to terminate a game, select the Reset option from the main menu. Once you reset the game, you may change an option, quit the game, etc.

The OS/2 Presentation Manager, Win 3.1, and Win 95 versions play just as tough but look much cooler. The Win versions have a very useful replay feature which highlights the moves that are learned. The archives are:

OS/2 (PM)	`trickle.zip`
Win16 (Win 3.1)	`trick16.zip`
Win32 (Win 95)	`trick32.zip`

They can be found as freeware on the Internet. Have fun!

LEN and NARENDRA
ldorfman@li.net